THE
DEVELOPMENT
OF
MOTIVES
AND VALUES
IN THE CHILD

᪥

BASIC TOPICS IN PSYCHOLOGY

Edwin G. Boring, EDITOR

SOCIAL PSYCHOLOGY

LEONARD BERKOWITZ
The Development of Motives and Values in the Child

ARTHUR R. COHEN
Attitude Change and Social Influence

MORTON DEUTSCH AND ROBERT M. KRAUSS
Theories in Social Psychology

BERTRAM H. RAVEN
Interpersonal Relations and Behavior in Groups

THE DEVELOPMENT OF MOTIVES AND VALUES IN THE CHILD

Leonard Berkowitz

Basic Books, Inc.

PUBLISHERS

NEW YORK : LONDON

ACKNOWLEDGMENTS

THANKS are due to Harper & Row, for their permission to quote from A. H. Maslow, *Motivation and Personality,* and to McGraw-Hill Book Co., for permission to reprint excerpts from L. Berkowitz, *Aggression: A Social Psychological Analysis.*

EDITOR'S FOREWORD

THE ENORMOUS GROWTH of scientific research and activity since World War II has included psychology as one of the recognized life sciences. Psychology now makes no small contribution to the rapid change in Western culture and civilization, a contribution that consists of a stream of new discoveries. There is also to be remembered, however, psychology's contribution to its own maintenance. That lies in teaching, for every academic generation must train the next. The roots of psychology must grow if the branches are to spread and the seeds of new growth germinate in the classroom. Research would ultimately exhaust itself were adequate prior training of the scientists deficient. That fact is now well recognized in principle, if not always in practice.

These short books are designed, in the first place, to make instruction easier. The ablest instructor is inevitably an individualist. He is never content to design his course to fit the idiosyncrasies of the other able man who wrote his textbook. A single text, moreover, seldom contains enough material to constitute all the reading a student needs. The instructor will wish to supplement his text and lectures and to have freedom in choosing what he shall add. The availability of many small books packed with solid reading enables the instructor to choose what he wants and makes their purchase by the student practicable.

The other use of these books is to satisfy the intellectual curiosity of intelligent laymen. They are not so technical that professional men and thinking women who are keeping an eye on the advance of civilization cannot use them to understand what the psychologists think and know. The philosopher, the historian, the lawyer, the physician, and the modern mother of grown children can surely employ these books in keeping up with the scientific times.

Since World War II, psychology has been expanding in many directions, forming connections with social science, on the one side, and with biological and physical science, on the other. It has thus been said to be both "sociotropic" and "biotropic" as it turns now toward social science, now toward biological science. Scientific biology is older than scientific sociology, and thus biotropic psychology is older than sociotropic. As a consequence of its youth, scientific social psychology is at present less sure of itself than is physiological psychology or psychophysics, and for that reason Basic Topics in Social Psychology tend to stress the way in which facts are a function of method, to discuss how the facts were obtained, and sometimes to present contradictory findings. Such contradictions are no fault of the author, but rather that of the youthfulness of this science. With social psychology still waiting on maturity, these books give their readers an insight into a science that is still growing up.

Edwin G. Boring

CONTENTS

THE
DEVELOPMENT
OF
MOTIVES
AND VALUES
IN THE CHILD

I

INTRODUCTION

RATHER THAN casting its net widely, this book will try to provide an intensive review of two somewhat specific topics: achievement motivation and morality. There need be no apologies for the selection of these aspects of social behavior. In essence, what we are here concerned with is socialization—the process by which children learn to become adult members of their society. Given the present social order—with its emphasis on technological advance, its Horatio-Alger ideal of social mobility, and its hopes for responsible and moral behavior by the individual—what could be more appropriate than a discussion of the motives, values, and attitudes intimately involved in these matters?

The focus on achievement motivation and morality does not, of course, preclude consideration of a wide variety of factors which are generally important in the socialization process. We will examine the effects of a number of conditions which impinge on the child—his culture, religion, and social class; the examples his mother and father set him; and the manner in which he is disciplined. In this discussion, furthermore, some attention will be given to the role of the child's identification with his parents and to how motives and values operate in governing behavior. A great many social influences determine how hard the individual will work just for the sake of doing well or how concerned he will be to avoid moral transgressions, and many of these influences affect the development and operation of other motives and values as well.

Though this survey will offer no concrete advice to parents, educators, or politicians, some lessons can perhaps be drawn from the material we will cover. The findings in many of the studies add up, for the writer at least, to one important point: the parent who wants his child to be reasonably successful (as success is ordinarily defined in our society) and a responsible and law-abiding citizen apparently has to take an active part in developing appropriate values and motives in the child. He cannot merely indulge his child's wishes, hoping the child will then automatically develop the desired motives and values. These aims and beliefs evidently have to be deliberately inculcated in the youngster. They will not necessarily arise just because the child's needs have been gratified and he has been sheltered from frustrations.

How Should the Child Be Treated?

If modern parents are confused as to how they should bring up their children, part of the blame can be attributed to the changes in the advice given them by "experts" in the past thirty or so years (Brim, 1959; Bronfenbrenner, 1958; Miller & Swanson, 1958; Wolfenstein, 1953). In the period between the two world wars, physicians, educators, and psychologists typically urged parents to impose a regular if not rigid discipline on their offspring. Children could easily go off on paths of wickedness or error, it was believed. If they were not potentially evil, they were at least so malleable that they could easily be "spoiled" and develop bad habits. Parents should therefore be firm. The child should never be permitted to dominate his mother and father. He should be fed on schedule and weaned, trained, and fed solid foods at a definite time regardless of the resistance he might show. Should the parents give in to his cries and desires, he would grow up to be an uncivil, demanding "monster."

The 1940's witnessed a drastic departure from this rigid approach to child rearing. Strongly influenced by psychoanalytic writings, many experts seemed to fear more than anything else that the child might develop neurotic inhibitions. Instead of warning against spoiling the child, these authorities now cautioned the parent against overrestraining him. Not only did the child need care and attention, but, they insisted, harsh frustrations could result in the persistence of infantile wishes. Mildness and permissiveness were the order of the day.

With the 1950's, however, the pendulum has swung back somewhat (Bronfenbrenner, 1958; Wolfenstein, 1953). There has been a return to restraints, if only halfheartedly. Many prominent writers in the field of child training now suggest that the parent impose some limits on his child. Love and attention are certainly necessary, they state, but the child should not be gratified continually. Furthermore, he is too young to understand the dangers of the street, stairs, and stove. He must be controlled for his own protection and because other people also have needs.

Where do we now stand? It is probably fair to say that there are two somewhat opposing doctrines of child training in existence today. Contemporary descendants of Freud as well as present-day behaviorists generally agree on the necessity of both loving and training the child. In contrast, other theorists, such as Kurt Goldstein, Erich Fromm, Abraham Maslow, and Carl Rogers, place greater emphasis on gratifying the child's needs. These two approaches should be spelled out in greater detail; there is a good possibility, as I suggested earlier, that the latter doctrine, if followed seriously, would actually impede the development of the motives and values with which we are mainly concerned.

Gratification is not enough. Although many specialists in child rearing have advocated extreme permissiveness in the name of Sigmund Freud, Freud himself thought that some frustration is necessary for both individual personality development and an effective social order. For one thing, he proposed that the ego, the personality's executive agency, has its origin in the thwarting of the infant's wishes. The ego presumably cannot deal adequately with the frustrations of adult life unless it has been strengthened by encountering and overcoming occasional frustrations in the individual's formative years.

But, more than this, Freud also believed, society itself rests ultimately on restraint and force. He condoned the repressiveness of society in various ways, assuming that the individual's desires are often opposed to social interests. War, he told Albert Einstein (Freud, 1932), has its roots in an innate aggressive drive. Man supposedly has an instinctive urge to destroy either himself or others. Given this drive, brute violence can only be controlled by the power of the organized community. Right is essentially the might of a community. Similarly, the irrational urges and weaknesses of the masses often justify powerful leaders and strong social controls. According to one recent commentator (Rieff, 1961, Ch. 7),

Freud definitely did not look at coercion as only the result of defective social organization. Some restraint and force, he believed, is necessary for the well-being of society.

Few psychoanalysts today share Freud's conception of an innate destructive drive (cf. Berkowitz, 1962). Nevertheless, most contemporary Freudians favor some direct parental control and supervision of the child. Love and attention are imperative, but adequate superego and ego development theoretically require some parental frustrations and admonitions. According to psychoanalytic formulations, the superego—the constellation of moral and ideal standards within the personality—arises primarily through the child's identification with parental figures. "The outstanding identification," says Fenichel (1945, p. 104), "takes place with that parent who was regarded as the source of the decisive frustrations."

Although psychoanalytic theory places particular stress on the child's identification, with the parental figure largely responsible for the thwarting of his Oedipal desires, recent behavioral research suggests that youngsters often model themselves after adults who are capable of frustrating them (have the power to reward and punish them) in various ways (Bandura, Ross, & Ross, 1963). Thus, young boys evidently identify with their fathers most readily—at least in the sense of adopting the masculine role—when the fathers generally are both nurturant and punitive (Mussen & Distler, 1959). The parent who would have his child copy him should be able to control and punish the child as well as love and nurture him.

More than just thwarting the child, parental standards define "right" and "wrong" for him when he is too young to understand the difference. Admonitions and demands imposed on the child are therefore also vitally important in the formation of the child's conscience (Munroe, 1955, p. 210). Similarly, parental standards probably have an important part in the origin of ambition (Blum, 1953, p. 113). Psychoanalytic theory definitely regards the mother and father as doing much to shape the child's motives and ideals.

Modern behaviorists have a somewhat similar conception of child rearing. Like the psychoanalysts, they believe that the child has to learn to behave in a socially adaptive manner. Both schools also contend that most of the motives involved in social behavior are derived from a smaller number of biological drives. Moreover, both groups point out that the acquisition of inner controls—inhibitions—is an important aspect of the socialization process. Parental figures are often instrumental in the development of such self-controlling mechanisms, they suggest, and they hold that the child's imitation of or identification with his mother and father generally has a major part in the acquisition of both social motives and self-restraints (cf. Bandura & Walters, 1963).

Self-actualization and child development. The opposing doctrine of child rearing with which we shall be concerned manifests a much greater faith in the intrinsic goodness of human nature. It maintains that an inherent "growth process," or self-actualizing tendency, would lead man inevitably into paths of creativity and genuine morality if the child's basic needs were not thwarted in the course of his growing up.

Such a conception is usually associated with neo-Freudian or *Gestalt*-phenomenological theorists, such as Fromm, Goldstein, and Maslow. In actuality, however, it dates back to the romantic notions of the late eighteenth and early nineteenth centuries. Many of the French *philosophes* also assumed that goodness was inherent in the original state of man. If society's frustrations could be eliminated, they argued, Europeans would be as good as the "noble savage" living in the unspoiled wilds of the New World. Their twentieth-century counterparts also seem to believe that everything desirable will follow from the elimination of social frustrations, particularly in the individual's formative years.

A. H. Maslow (1954) has been one of the foremost exponents of the growth-through-gratification doctrine. Putting it simply, Maslow posits a hierarchy of needs, with less potent needs emerging on gratification of the more potent ones. The physiological needs (e.g., hunger, thirst, sex) dominate the organism when they are unsatisfied. Gratification of these presumably allows the next higher set of needs, the safety needs, to emerge and organize the personality. If these desires are met in turn, the needs of love, affection, and belongingness would supposedly arise. Finally, with the satisfaction of these needs and after the person has gratified his desires for esteem, a new source of discontent will arise—the need for self-actualization. The individual seeks self-fulfillment; what he can be, he must be (p. 91). Complete satisfaction of a lower-order need is supposedly not necessary before the higher-order desires can emerge, but any degree of thwarting of the lower, more potent, need is said to interfere with the full unfolding of the higher-order drives (pp. 100 f.).

Maslow is explicit: psychological health theoretically increases with increasing need gratification (p. 115). According to his formulation, the healthy organism, being need-gratified and thereby released for self-actualization, develops according to its intrinsic growth tendencies rather than being affected by environmental conditions. It is the neurotic organism, lacking satisfactions from the external environment, which is shaped by the environment more than by its own inherent nature (p. 116). If a child were to experience constant gratification of his emerging needs, such an analysis suggests, he would be *less* and not more likely to become psychopathic.

As strange to the lay reader as such a conception might be, Freudian theory actually interprets psychopathic behavior in a somewhat similar vein. The psychopath who cannot restrain his urges has a poorly developed superego, supposedly because of inadequate identification with parental figures. For one reason or another, the individual had insufficient affectional ties with his mother and father or other adults when he was a young child and therefore failed to adopt appropriate adult standards (Munroe, 1955, pp. 292 f.). There is some relevant empirical evidence on this point. Many hyperaggressive youngsters who exhibit frequent hostility and relatively little self-control have suffered serious thwartings, particularly of their needs for love and dependency, in the early years of their life (Bandura & Walters, 1959; Berkowitz, 1962). All are agreed on the detrimental effects of too little love in the child's early, formative years. But are love and gratification enough to ensure adequate social development?

For Maslow and others, the self-actualizing tendency, if not blocked by other, frustration-induced and less mature, inclinations, is an unerring path to morality. The self-actualized person, says Fromm (1947), follows a rational policy of self-interest. He acts, not in terms of a subjective feeling of what his interest is, but more objectively in pursuit of the full development of his potentialities. Self-realization is supposedly identical with virtue. Fromm believes that the psychoanalytic superego is basically an authoritarian conscience, since it is derived from external agents. The contents of such a conscience stem from the dictates and taboos of authority, whereas its strength rests on fear of and admiration for authority. A person with an authoritarian conscience feels good when he believes he will be approved by the authority and guilty when he thinks he will be disapproved. In contrast, the humanistic conscience of the self-realized individual is the inner voice of the person himself seeking fulfillment and productivity. The guilt feelings of this latter conscience arise when the self goes unfulfilled.

Maslow (1954) contends that self-actualizing people know

the difference between right and wrong, but says that "their notions of right and wrong are often not the conventional ones" (p. 221). Furthermore, "the self-actualizing person *practically never* [italics mine] allows convention to hamper him or inhibit him from doing anything that he considers very important or basic" (p. 209). Each man can be a law unto himself.

I think that we can gain a better understanding of the implications of this doctrine by considering the novels and writings of Ayn Rand. Her most popular novel, *The Fountainhead,* tells of a self-actualizing person, an architect, who pursues his artistic goals undeviatingly despite the scorn and interference of the less-fulfilled people around him. Following his self-interest, our hero rapes a woman at the beginning of the book and later, toward the end of the novel, deliberately destroys a low-cost housing project (for which he had been the architect) because the builders had departed from his plans. Altruism, Miss Rand insists, is the cardinal sin of our society.

Was the architect's behavior—supposedly oriented toward the fulfillment of his artistic potentialities—"identical with virtue"? When is the individual behaving in terms of his "real" self-interests? This question is a difficult one. Fromm maintains that the person who is ignorant of his self and its real needs can deceive himself as to what his real self-interest is, but such a statement provides little help. We are given no unequivocal criteria for distinguishing between behavior guided by self-realization and actions stemming from self-ignorance. In general, the growth-through-gratification view of child rearing is doubtful philosophically and highly questionable empirically. As one commentator (Ausubel, 1952, p. 396) has observed, Fromm's "psychological theory strays far from the conditions of human moral development." This doctrine is based essentially on impressionistic observations of a restricted sample of oversocialized people possessing extremely strong inhibitions. Just because they may be struggling against their excessive inner restraints does not necessarily mean that other people do not require at least some inhibitions or that some vague and unspecified "growth force" will ensure creativity and social progress and harmony.

We can and ought to ask whether certain kinds of child-rearing practices can facilitate social progress and promote domestic tranquility. The following pages summarize a number of empirical studies whose findings may help us decide how our children should be brought up. Such decisions should be based, at least in part, on carefully collected facts rather than on religioromantic speculations on the inherent nature of man.

2

ACHIEVEMENT MOTIVATION

Achievement Motivation and Technological Progress

Romantics often glorify "the good old days." Dissatisfied with the present state of society—a frequent accusation is that society places too much emphasis on materialistic matters to the neglect of spiritual concerns—many romantics dream of other times when men were supposedly far more noble than they are today. If they do not turn to earlier years for their inspiration, they sometimes look to other countries and other cultures. Generally, the more primitive the culture, the better. Modern society is supposed to spoil things. The peasant and primitive lead a simple and, hence, "good" life, whereas their more civilized counterparts are frustrated in the pursuit of ephemeral and "artificial" goals. The closer we can get to nature—or to the *philosophes'* "original state of man"—we are told, the better off we will be.

As an illustration of such a view, a noted writer in the field of social science once advised Mexican peasants to resist the spread of modern technology to their villages. They had something precious, they were informed, something the Western world was struggling to regain. They should maintain their "magnificent inertia" and conserve their way of life. If a new highway comes, they should buy "all the boxes of extra-sized carpet tacks" they could afford (Chase, 1931; cited in McClelland, 1961).

But, despite its good intent, there seems to be little inclination to heed such advice. Instead of fighting off the vehicles of technological progress with all the carpet tacks they can afford, many nations insist on new and better highways to smooth the path. It is not for us to say whether these desires are wise or the surest path to "ultimate happiness." But, whether wise or not, most of the countries of the world apparently want to emulate American technological progress. People everywhere seem to be convinced that they also want automobiles and television sets or at least washing machines and refrigerators. Rather than turning away from modern civilization, they ask how they, too, can achieve technological and economic advance.

An important and provocative book by David McClelland (1961) maintains that the motivations of the dominant members of a society play a major role in spurring economic and technological improvements. If a country is to accelerate its economic growth, it obviously has to break with those traditions impeding such growth. But, more than this, the society should also do everything possible to develop the appropriate motivations in its members.

"Naturally," many would say at this point. If people are to engage in those activities leading to technological advances, they have to believe they can make money by doing so. Capital must be available, and those with access to the capital must be convinced that they can earn a profit by investing their money, time, and effort in technological activities. Human motivation is fairly simple to the economic determinist, whether he is a Marxist or a capitalist: it is money and economic gain that make the world go 'round.

The eminent German sociologist Max Weber has shown, however, that such a formulation is at best an oversimplification. In his classic work on the Protestant ethic and capitalism, Weber (1930) pointed out that the early Calvinist businessman seemed to be concerned with more than just money. His religious beliefs prevented him from spending money on himself; he could not engage in self-indulgence and display. Why, then, did he work so hard and so long? In answer, Weber suggested (cf. McClelland, 1961, p. 47) that such a person works primarily for "the irrational sense of having done his job well." For McClelland, there was nothing strange about such satisfactions. He and his colleagues (McClelland, Atkinson, Clark, & Lowell, 1953) had been engaged for several years in studying what seemed to be just this type of instigation—the achievement motive.

In very simple terms, the achievement motive is generally regarded as the impetus to do well relative to some standard of excellence. A person with strong achievement needs wants to be successful at some challenging task, not for status or profit, but merely for the sake of doing well.

Measuring achievement motivation. The initial studies of this motive were carried out in the experimental laboratory (cf. Atkinson, 1958). McClelland and his co-workers began this research by first developing projective measures of the aroused need for achievement. Male college students wrote five-minute stories in response to scenes portrayed on cards (actually shown to them on slides) after being placed in one of two fundamentally different conditions. In some cases, the subjects constructed these stories after becoming concerned with how well they had worked on some preliminary tasks, i.e., with their achievement, whereas in other instances subjects responded to the slides after they were induced to have a more relaxed attitude toward their performance. The stories the subjects wrote were then analyzed for differences between the two main conditions, with the investigators assuming that such differences could be taken as signs of achievement motivation. In measuring individual differences in achievement motivation, then, people having many of these signs in their test protocols are regarded as being characteristically higher in achievement motivation than people with relatively few achievement signs.

Though most of the research on achievement motivation employs scores derived from stories told about pictorial scenes (i.e., on Thematic Apperception Test ["TAT"] or similar cards), other methods have also been used. For example, in one procedure, devised by Elizabeth French (Atkinson, 1958), subjects are given a sentence describing the behavior of some person and then asked to explain why the person acts in this fashion. These "explanations" are then coded in the same way as the TAT stories. Other, more exploratory, methods have also been employed (cf. Atkinson, 1958; McClelland, 1961), but we cannot discuss them here. It is important to note, however, that these "projective" indexes do not yield the same results as self-descriptive statements (Atkinson, 1958, p. 38). Those people who *say* that they often want to work hard and do well are apparently not necessarily highly motivated to expend effort for achievement.

Achievement motivation and behavior. How does the typical person with high achievement motivation behave? Several experiments indicate that such people often show a greater preference for moderately difficult tasks than do subjects with low achievement scores. But this preference for fairly difficult tasks does not necessarily arise out of a liking for gambling;

moderate risks are preferred primarily when skill or ability is involved. People with strong achievement needs have confidence in themselves, but they do not blithely assume that they are the darlings of fate. They trust themselves, rather than luck. However, even when their own skills are involved in the performance, they evidently do not become motivated to do well unless the task is challenging to them. According to McClelland, such persons generally become instigated to succeed at a given job when the task requires at least some "personal initiative, or even inventiveness, for solution" and thus offers some degree of challenge, rather than a complete assurance of winning (McClelland, 1961, pp. 212–224).

McClelland believed that the person with strong achievement motivation should be particularly suited for executive or entrepreneurial occupations (p. 210). Entrepreneurship, he pointed out, usually involves risk-taking. The entrepreneur must often make decisions under conditions of uncertainty. If his decision is successful, he may make a profit for himself or his firm or solve a problem facing his organization. But he has no guarantee that his proposal will work, and failure may be costly to himself or his organization. As an entrepreneur or executive, he has to know when a risk is a reasonable one and has to be willing to take a chance on the moderate odds.

An interesting study by Child, Storm, and Veroff (McClelland, 1961, pp. 64–68) indicated that a high level of achievement motivation in primitive societies is associated with full-time entrepreneurial occupations. These investigators selected twelve folk tales from forty-five primitive cultures and coded each story for signs of achievement motivation. The societies were also classified as to whether people in them engaged in full-time entrepreneurial activities—controlling production or producing more of something than the individual can consume himself in order to exchange the production for some form of income. (Traders and independent artisans are examples.) A significant relationship was obtained; even though the cultures varied over a wide range of economic and social systems, the groups high in achievement motivation, as indicated by their folk tales, were much more likely than the low achievement groups to have such entrepreneurial occupations.

Before going on to the relationship between achievement motivation and economic growth, two other points made by McClelland are worth considering. First, though a person with high achievement motivation may be suited for the entrepreneurial role (provided that he has the intelligence and other necessary personality qualities), he may not seek out business occupations if they are too easy to enter. Generalizing from previous research (cf. Atkinson, 1958, pp. 322–339), we would expect the achievement-oriented person to prefer relatively difficult jobs; people high in achievement motivation tend to favor challenging and moderately difficult activities. Thus, where a middle-class or perhaps even lower-class youngster with strong achievement motivation might be drawn to a business career because such an occupation is fairly difficult of attainment, a boy from an upper-class family might find entry into business much too easy. If he is highly motivated to do well, he might then turn to the professions (McClelland, 1961, pp. 243–253). In support of this analysis, one investigator has reported that liking for a given occupation in a middle-class Japanese sample was a function of both the individual's achievement motivation and the difficulty (defined in terms of prestige) of the occupation (pp. 247 f.). A person with strong achievement desires will seek out those careers representing the optimal degree of challenge for him. He will want moderate risk rather than complete certainty of entry into the field.

Second, McClelland also suggests why the achievement-oriented person may at times be interested in monetary rewards for his endeavors. A business executive with strong needs for achievement may not work primarily for all the good things money can bring him, but he is not oblivious to the value of money. Economic gain can be important indeed to such a person; it serves primarily as a symbol of attainment, a measure of his success (pp. 236 f.). The achievement-oriented individual does not have to be working for himself or to be a free agent who is master of his fate in order to gratify his achievement needs. He does, however, want to accomplish something worthwhile, and money can function as the concrete sign that he *has* done well (pp. 229–234).

Other research has pointed to yet another important characteristic of the person with strong achievement needs: an ability to defer pleasures. Trinidadian Negro children scoring high on the TAT measure of achievement motivation were more willing than children with low achievement scores to put off getting a reward in order to obtain a larger reward in the future (Mischel, 1961b).

All in all, a variety of research findings provide reasons why achievement motivation may be an important factor in economic advancement. Summarizing, we can say that the individual with a strong need to achieve is highly motivated to succeed when performance has "achievement significance" for him, and he is willing and able to take risks in order to reach his goals. With other factors constant, a society containing many people with such characteristics is surely likely to have a fairly rapid rate of economic and technological growth.

Testing the economic-growth hypothesis. How can such a hypothesis be tested? Ideally, of course, measures of achievement motivation should be obtained from representative samples of the people in a number of nations, and these measures could then be correlated with various economic indexes. Such a procedure would, however, obviously be extremely expensive. No one group of social-science investigators possesses either the financial or professional resources for such an ambitious undertaking. As an alternative, McClelland obtained children's readers from a group of non-tropical countries for the periods 1920–1929 (twenty-three nations) and 1946–1955 (forty nations), assuming that the stories in these books represented the public concerns of the people in a country. Twenty-one stories from the readers of each of these countries were then analyzed for signs of achievement motivation, as well as for certain other values and motives.

The principal index of technological advancement employed by McClelland was the deviation in the country's gain in electrical output during a given period from what might be expected from the country's prior level of output. That is, the countries having a high level of electrical production (per capita) at the beginning of a given period characteristically had a greater gain in output by the end of the period than the nations starting with a lower level of electrical production. The rich get richer. Some of these countries, however, showed a greater gain than was to be expected from this general trend, and other countries had a slower increase in electrical output. The researchers then sought to determine whether these differences from expectation were due, at least in part, to the level of achievement motivation in the nation, as indicated by the children's readers.

McClelland (1961, Ch. 3) obtained the correlations he had predicted. The need-achievement scores for the nations in the 1925-period sample were positively and significantly correlated with the technological growth scores for the years 1929–1950. The greater the concern for achievement in a nation, the greater was its above-expectation gain in electrical output in the years immediately following. (This relationship also held when damage during World War II was taken into account.) Note that the achievement level evidently preceded economic growth. Thus, the achievement scores derived from the 1950-period readers were not significantly correlated with technological advancement in the prior years. These motivational measures from the 1950 period were, however, related to above-expectation gain in electrical production for the years 1952–1958. Achievement concerns, as indicated by the children's stories, come before or parallel—and perhaps contribute to—economic growth, but they do not seem to be the result of such growth (at least not of the growth of the immediately preceding years) in any simple fashion. The motive scores are uncorrelated with *previous* growth, but are related to *subsequent* growth.

Developing Achievement Motivation

If McClelland's thesis is correct, societies wanting rapid economic and technological advancement must be concerned with developing a high level of achievement motivation in many of their people. What are the conditions that give rise to such motivation?

Cultural factors. Though the concern with achievement reflected in the children's readers may not be merely a reaction to periods of economic boom, it may mirror, at least in part, the "mood or motivational level" of a nation at the given time (p. 101). A nation's motivational mood is subject to change. Countries high in achievement motivation in the 1925 period were not necessarily still high in the 1950's. McClelland's analysis suggests that France and Germany rose from a below-average achievement level in 1925 to somewhat above the mean of the sample by the 1950's, while the motivation scores from Sweden, Denmark, and Great Britain decreased to below the sample mean in this period (p. 90).

The scores for the United States remained high in McClelland's sample, but other investigators, employing a similar procedure, have indicated that Americans should not be complacent (assuming that they value achievement motivation). DeCharms and Moeller (1962) analyzed fourth-grade children's readers from this country, using books representing each twenty-year period from 1800 to 1952. They reported that achievement imagery rose from 1800 to 1890 and thereafter went into a fairly sharp decline. Supporting the contention that achievement motivation contributes to technological progress, achievement scores were highly and positively correlated with the number of patents granted per one million population in each twenty-year period.

We cannot say with any certainty why the level of achievement motivation in important groups in a nation should vary from time to time. One good possibility is that these groups have had it too easy. McClelland here draws a fascinating connection between the research on achievement motivation and Toynbee's discussion of the role of "optimal challenges" in the rise of civilizations, a hypothesis which is also relevant to the thesis of growth through gratification. People with strong achievement motivation, it will be recalled, tend to work hardest when given moderately difficult tasks. Moderate risks could activate the achievement motives of the people in a society and may even be necessary for the continued strength of this instigation. If members of a society lack sufficiently difficult challenges, their concern with achievement might decline (pp. 339 f.).

Thus, a study of 104 societies (Barry, Child, & Bacon, 1959) found that those with little accumulated food, which therefore faced some hardships, tended to train their children to be assertive to a greater extent than societies having great stores of accumulated food. This training in assertiveness could well foster achievement motivation. Whether or not such training in assertiveness is important, continued and easy gratification of our every whim could lessen ardor to do well for its own sake. We may require occasional challenges and periodic difficulties and frustrations so that, by overcoming them, we can obtain the satisfaction of a task well done. Without these challenges and the satisfaction of having worked successfully, achievement motivation could weaken.

As another possibility, Riesman (1950) has proposed that American society, under the influence of population growth and educational philosophies, is creating more and more "other-directed" personalities. If such a change is occurring, it might produce a concomitant decline in achievement motivation, perhaps through increasing the level of affiliation motivation—a need for pleasant social relationships with other people. DeCharms and Moeller observed that affiliation imagery generally increased in the American readers from 1800 to 1930, as Riesman's thesis would have predicted. However, there was an unforeseen drop in concern with affiliation in the readers for the 1950 period. To add to the confusion, McClelland (1961) reported that achievement motivation, as inferred from his sample of readers, was negatively and significantly correlated with affiliation motivation only in the 1950's. Affiliative concern may have inhibited achievement motivation only in more recent times (p. 166).

Whatever is happening at the cultural level, other research (Moss & Kagan, 1961) indicates that the level of achievement motivation in an individual is fairly stable between early childhood and adulthood. In this investigation, one psychologist rated the level of achievement motivation characteristically displayed during childhood by each of seventy-one adult males and females on the basis of observations of them made when they were children, before knowledge of the subject's

adult behavior was available. A second psychologist interviewed each person, now twenty to twenty-nine years of age,
and rated each without having the childhood information. It
was found that the ratings of strivings for achievement at six
years of age (but not for the younger years) were positively
and significantly correlated with ratings of similar behavior in
adulthood. In addition, achievement imagery given in response
to TAT cards administered at about fourteen years of age
reliably predicted adult achievement behavior (cf. also Kagan
& Moss, 1959). Achievement strivings exhibited during the
first four years of school evidently are a good index of later
achievement behavior in adolescence and adulthood. But, although a father might have strong concern with achievement
throughout his lifetime, his son will not necessarily have the
same ambition, for the father may have made things too easy
for the boy.

Religious influences. McClelland started his research into
the motivational bases of economic growth by generalizing
from Weber's (1930) pioneering analysis of the relation between capitalism and Protestantism. Protestantism, with its
emphasis on hard work, asceticism, and self-reliance for salvation, presumably had a major role in the rise of capitalism
and the industrial growth of England, Germany, Switzerland,
and the Scandinavian countries. In essence, the Protestant
Reformation insisted that the individual could and should seek
his spiritual salvation by his own efforts, rather than through
the intervention of such priestly authorities as the Catholic
Church. Since the individual was to be self-reliant in seeking
salvation, he was supposedly the readier to accept individual
initiative in other areas of life as well.

Following this lead, McClelland (1955) at first conjectured
that Protestantism, by training its people to be relatively independent, had fostered the development of achievement mo-

tivation which impelled a rapid level of economic and technological growth. Later observations, however, indicate that Protestantism in and of itself is not necessarily more favorable to economic development than any form of Catholicism. Progress may require more than a motivation to succeed. Technological and economic advances may depend on particular values, as well as on a drive for achievement in important group members, and we will also have to determine how prevalent certain values in each of the major religious denominations are.

There is some indirect evidence that Protestants may have stronger needs for achievement than Catholics. Using percapita consumption of electric power (corrected for natural resources) as his index of economic status, McClelland (1961, pp. 50–53) showed that, for twenty-four temperate-zone countries, Protestant countries typically were above average and Catholic countries were below average. These data were collected, however, in 1950. Given the rapid economic development in France and Italy and the decreased rate of growth in England and Scandinavia in recent years, the difference obtained by McClelland may now be much less or perhaps even abolished. Also—presumably indicating religious group differences in achievement motivation—American Catholics on the average are lower in social status than either Protestants or Jews. In many cases, these differences are due to such factors as their relatively recent migration to this country. Nevertheless, even when these sociological variables affecting economic attainment are held constant, Jews and most Protestant denominations characteristically far exceed the Catholics in economic standing (Mayer & Sharp, 1962). Catholics are apparently less likely to attain worldly success than are most other religious groups in this country even when all start off on the same sociological footing.

Other evidence suggests, furthermore, that the McClelland-

Weber analysis may also be valid in non-Western societies. According to Child, Storm, and Veroff (1958; cited in Mc-Clelland, 1961, pp. 70, 371), achievement level as it is inferred from folk tales tends to be relatively low when a society also believes that people can communicate with their sacred beings only through the mediation of special religious authorities or experts. Achievement motivation appears to be fairly weak in a society in which its people cannot reach the Divine Being by means of their individual activities.

More direct observations of the level of achievement motivation in the major religious groups have, however, yielded conflicting results. The first studies conducted in New England (e.g., Rosen, 1959) tended to corroborate McClelland's initial expectations; but, when achievement measures were obtained for the first time from a representative sample of American adults, it was found that, though Jewish men on the average had the highest achievement-motivation scores, high motivation scores were somewhat more prevalent in *Catholic* than in Protestant men (Veroff, Feld, & Gurin, 1962). Catholics everywhere are not necessarily lower than Protestants in achievement needs. It may be that New England Catholics, constituting a larger proportion of the population in their area, have been slower to adopt the aspirations of the American "core culture" than their less-traditional coreligionists in other parts of the country.

The Protestant ethic. If the average American Catholic is not necessarily lower in achievement motivation than the typical Protestant, he still is likely to possess somewhat different values. The attitudes and orientations widely shared in the Catholic group may contribute to the low rate of upward social mobility in this denomination (Lenski, 1961).

Our analysis of Protestant–Catholic differences in values must begin with Weber's pioneering insights. Although the

Calvinist believed that he was predestined for salvation, Weber pointed out, he also had to behave in a particular manner in order to acknowledge the position into which he had been born. In addition to being self-reliant, he had to avoid idle luxuries, accept asceticism, and work hard at the role to which he had been assigned by God. If he came to prefer these values, he held what is commonly known as "the Protestant ethic." Extrapolating from Weber's discussion, several authorities (cf. Lenski, 1961) have suggested that, in contrast to Catholics, Protestants are more prone to insist that a person should (1) be independent in reaching his important individual goals and (2) attempt to actively manipulate his environment, rather than passively accepting his fate.

Catholics as a group evidently place less importance on independence, particularly for children, than do Protestants, although parents belonging to both denominations may train their children to be self-reliant in various activities at a relatively early age. McClelland, following Weber's lead, at first predicted that Protestant mothers and fathers would be quicker than their Catholic counterparts to train their children to be independent. Here, again, the first studies making use of New England mothers yielded supporting evidence (McClelland, 1961, pp. 358 f.; Rosen, 1959); but later research based on a national sample of adults (Veroff, Atkinson, Feld, & Gurin, 1960; cited in McClelland, pp. 358 f.) failed to obtain similar differences between the religious groups. Nevertheless, though they may resemble Protestants in the age at which they want their children to be self-reliant, Catholics in general do not value intellectual independence as much as do Protestants.

Findings from intensive studies in Detroit document these group differences in attitudes toward independence (Lenski, 1961). As we might expect, Catholic parents were less likely than either white Protestant or Jewish parents to believe that a twelve-year-old child should be allowed to decide for himself whether he would go to church or Sunday school (p. 234). The group differences, however, extended beyond religious matters. When asked what the most important things for a child to learn were, most of the adults placed special stress on intellectual autonomy (learning to think for himself) and obedience; but, within each social class, Protestants and Jews were more inclined to favor intellectual independence over obedience than were Catholics. Catholics were apparently somewhat less concerned whether their children learned to think for themselves (p. 222).

There is also reason to believe that Catholics have, on the whole, a relatively fatalistic and passive attitude toward life. In separate studies conducted in New England (Rosen, 1959) and in West Germany (McClelland, 1961)—where Catholics are thoroughly integrated into the national culture—mothers were asked whether they agreed with such statements as: "When a man is born, the success he is going to have is already in the cards, so he might just as well accept it and not fight against it," and "Planning only makes a person unhappy, since your plans hardly ever work out anyway." Whether they lived in New England or in West Germany, more Catholic than Protestant mothers agreed with the statements. The Catholic women seemed to have a more passively fatalistic and "present-oriented" attitude toward life.

Detroit Catholics have also been found to have a more passive orientation toward economic attainment than their white Protestant or Jewish peers. In both the middle and the working classes, a smaller proportion of Catholics than of non-Catholics said that a workingman's children had a good chance of becoming well-to-do and that ability was more important than family connections in determining success in life (Lenski, 1961, pp. 104 f.). What happens to a person, more of the Catholics appeared to be saying, is largely due to factors beyond his control. For them, man is not master of his fate.

Perhaps because of such attitudinal differences, Protestants generally have a greater interest in reading, higher education (cf. McClelland, 1961, pp. 320 f.), science, and individual inquiry than do Catholics, although probably not in classical humanistic education. Thus, Protestant colleges have turned out more eminent men of science relative to population than have Catholic institutions (p. 359). In some cases, of course, a fatalistic, accepting attitude can result in more adequate behavior. For instance, a study of mothers of retarded children indicated that Catholic women seemed to be more accepting of their handicapped offspring than were non-Catholic mothers, perhaps because the former, being more fatalistic, also absolved themselves of personal guilt for their children's condition (Zuk, Miller, Bartram, & Kling, 1961). The person who believes that he is master of his fate can feel guilty when given a cruel blow by forces beyond his control. He may think that he is somehow at fault. Fatalism would comfort him.

McClelland theorized that many of the attitudes and values that belong under the term "Protestant ethic" facilitate the development of achievement motivation. Indeed, he suggested that the Protestant Reformation represents only a special case "of a general increase in achievement motivation produced by an ideological change" (McClelland, 1961, p. 391). In his research into the correlates of economic growth, McClelland noted that some of the values typically associated with Protestantism are more characteristic of rapidly growing societies than of nations exhibiting slower technological development. A positive valuation of hard work, for example, though not significantly correlated with high scores in the achievement motive, was found more often in the readers from the rapidly developing countries than in those from the slowly growing nations (p. 189).

However, valuing hard work does not in itself necessarily lead to technological advance. Two sociologists (Goldstein &

Eichhorn, 1961) recently studied some 260 Midwestern farmers, comparing those who placed a great value on hard work to those who were less work-oriented. The men strongly favoring hard work were also more ascetic and individualistic than the other farmers, as we would expect from the notion of the Protestant ethic, but they also seemed more strongly bound to their farming traditions. They therefore did not make sufficient use of available technical information. Even though they worked hard, their strong traditionalism interfered with rational economic behavior. Achievement motivation and hard work cannot overcome "the dead hand of the past."

In summary, we may say that classic Protestantism evidently was more favorable to economic growth than was traditional Catholicism because of Protestantism's greater emphasis on asceticism, hard work, self-reliance, and independent achievement and because of its activistic orientation toward life. Modern Catholicism, however, may well be less tradition-bound than its historic counterpart, for many Catholics today do possess the beliefs that facilitate rapid technological development.

Minority-group status. Ever since the Middle Ages and perhaps even longer, Jews have been both castigated and praised for their economic success. Through the centuries, widely held stereotypes have pictured Jews as being unusually—and often unfairly—successful in financial matters. There is little doubt that today American Jews as a group have done well economically in comparison to other denominations. Thus, a previously cited study of various religious groups in Detroit (Mayer & Sharp, 1962) showed that, when the denominations were placed on an "equal footing" with respect to certain sociological factors fostering high economic attainment, Jews, followed by Episcopalians and Calvinists, had achieved the greatest worldly success. In part reflecting their high rate of upward social mobility (since many of them come from "new-immigrant" families), Jews have a far greater proportion in the nonmanual occupations (between 75 and 96 per cent in 1953) than the American population as a whole (38 per cent of the gainfully employed in 1950; Glazer, 1957). Along with this worldly success, Jews frequently are regarded as "shrewd," "mercenary," and "industrious" (Katz & Braly, 1933), and many undoubtedly do possess these traits.

Various explanations have been offered for both the high level of economic success attained by Jews and their personality characteristics. One explanation that has probably been advanced as often as any other attributes the "Jewish" qualities to the Jew's historical, precarious minority-group status. Being insecure in their marginal social position, Jews, it is suggested, try hard to compensate; they work hard to achieve security and to assert their worth. Such an analysis probably has a good deal of merit. Some "Jewish" personality traits may well be the result of insecurity stemming from minority status. For instance, a survey of all the psychiatric patients in New Haven, Connecticut, in 1950 (Myers & Roberts, 1957) found that Jews had a higher rate of neurosis than either Catholics or Protestants, presumably because Jews are under greater strain than either of the other groups.

But, as for economic attainment, McClelland (1961, p. 339) contends that a group's economic response to its marginal position depends, at least in part, on its level of achievement motivation. If its achievement motivation is strong, the marginal social position becomes a challenge to be met with vigorous effort. On the other hand, if the group has relatively weak needs for achievement, the inferior social position can be so much of a handicap that it leads to withdrawal.

There is little doubt that American Jews typically want to succeed in their tasks and do well in life. The national survey of group differences in achievement motivation (Veroff et al.,

1962) noted that high achievement motivation occurred most frequently in Jewish men. According to McClelland's analysis, there are both religious and family reasons for this strong motivation. For one thing, Judaism prescribes an individualistic approach to God. (This is the kind of religious approach that is characteristic of primitive cultures high in achievement motivation.) Rabbis, properly speaking, are teachers rather than necessary mediators between the individual and the Divine Being (McClelland, 1961, pp. 370 f.).

However, in addition to prescribing religious self-reliance (cf. also Glazer, 1957), Jewish culture frequently develops the kind of family life that is conducive to the creation of a high level of achievement motivation (McClelland, 1961, p. 364). Observations suggest that American Jewish families often set high levels of aspiration for their children. Mothers lavish a great deal of love and attention on their sons at the same time that they encourage them to do well. Moreover, the father's being characteristically nonauthoritarian and often less dominant than the mother does not inhibit the son's aspirations (cf. Strodtbeck, 1957). Thus, the young Jew's experiences in his family as he grows to manhood may actually contribute more to the development of his typically strong achievement desires than does his minority status.

Social class. We have good reason to expect a relationship between achievement motivation and social class, at least in American society. Two decades ago, Davis (1944) pointed out that middle-class youngsters are generally subjected to relatively strong social pressures to do well both in school and in later life. These adolescents should have comparatively strong achievement needs to the extent that they internalize such pressures. Similarly, Florence Kluckhohn (Kluckhohn & Strodtbeck, 1961) has also suggested that achievement motivation should flourish in the middle class. Not only does this "core culture" stress the importance of accomplishments and doing well, but, in contrast to both the upper- and lower-class groups, middle-class culture is also more likely to emphasize other values facilitating the development of achievement needs. Thus, Kluckhohn has characterized American middle-class culture as possessing a "future-doing" orientation. Families from this social stratum supposedly teach their sons to look to the future when they will do well and surpass their fathers' occupational levels.

In support of the Kluckhohn analysis, a study of Harvard freshmen (McArthur, 1955) demonstrated that men from middle-class public schools told more achievement-oriented stories in response to a TAT card than did upper-class, private-school-educated men. The wealthier group's stories contained strong indications of a "past" orientation, prescribing the father as a model for the son, as well as a "being" or "being-in-becoming" orientation, which emphasize self-fulfillment rather than accomplishments.

Empirical comparisons of middle- and lower-class groups have usually found stronger needs for achievement in the former. When the TAT was administered to boys residing in four Northeastern states (Rosen, 1959; Rosen, 1961), youngsters from the middle and upper social levels generally obtained higher achievement scores than did lower-class boys. In addition, the nationwide survey of achievement motivation cited earlier (Veroff et al., 1960) noted that the percentage of adult men with above-median achievement scores on the projective test was greater the higher the (1) educational and (2) occupational level of the group. The relation between family income and achievement motivation was irregular, but men from families having an income greater than $5,000 typically had higher scores than the men from families with a lower income.

Other research conducted in laboratory situations also has

indicated that middle- and upper-class people characteristically have greater achievement motivation than their working-class counterparts. In the first of these laboratory investigations, Douvan (1956) gave Midwestern high school seniors a series of preliminary tasks after telling them either that good performers would receive a $10 prize ("material reward present") or that there would be no such prize ("material reward absent"). In order to arouse their motivation, they were then informed they had failed on these preliminary tasks, and a thematic projective test was administered. The experimenter found that the middle-class students obtained relatively high achievement scores on the projective test both when a material reward was present and when it was absent. They presumably had a strongly generalized achievement motivation that was readily aroused by the possibility of symbolic as well as concrete rewards. In contrast, the working-class youngsters tended to have strong achievement motivation (no different from the middle-class level) only when the material reward was present. They wanted to do well, apparently, only when there was something concrete "in it for them."

Consistent with these findings and employing behavioral measures, psychologists have also reported that, in comparison to working-class children, middle-class students exhibited less variation in performance (on a number-tracing task and on an IQ test) from one situation offering a cash reward for good work to another occasion when no such rewards were offered. Their performance was relatively constant, presumably because they were motivated by symbolic as well as by tangible rewards. The lower-class students, on the other hand, were more likely to show good performance only when a material reward was present (Hoffman, Mitsos, & Protz, 1958). Essentially comparable results were obtained on a discrimination-learning task (Terrell, Durkin, & Wiesley, 1959).

Despite these findings, we must be careful not to generalize such social class differences too far. Middle- and upper-class people in some other societies may generally have relatively low achievement motivation. In Brazil, for example, boys from the bottom of the social hierarchy seem to have stronger achievement needs than boys from the highest stratum, possibly because the latter are excessively pampered and indulged (Rosen, 1962).

In our own society, furthermore, occupational categories may be just as important as social level per se in shaping motives and values. Miller and Swanson (1958) maintain that the entrepreneurial classes should be differentiated from the bureaucratic classes. The entrepreneurial middle class—composed of people who are self-employed or who are concerned with obtaining a profit, fee, or commission—is supposedly more likely to possess the values of the Protestant ethic than is the bureaucratic middle class, which obtains its livelihood primarily from large organizations. To buttress their analysis, Miller and Swanson reported differences in the child-rearing practices employed by entrepreneurial and bureaucratic mothers, with the former said to place greater emphasis on self-control and self-denial. We should certainly not make the mistake of thinking that a person who grew up in any part of the globe would necessarily have strong achievement desires just because he was an upper- or middle-class Protestant or Jew. His family, friends, associates, and even the culture of the region in which he lived all influence his motives and aspirations.

Social Mobility

Sociologists have at times described the social strata as relatively closed societies within which people associate primarily with others at their own level. ("The Cabots talk only to

Lowells, and Lowells speak only with God.") Such a conception is susceptible of exaggeration; it may neglect, for example, the possibility of people moving up or down in social status. Indeed, there is some evidence that class cultures, by fostering particular values and motives (such as achievement motivation), may affect the amount of social mobility shown by their members. This kind of class-influenced learning may be at least part of the reason why American business leaders have typically come from relatively prosperous families and why the working class has contributed proportionately few business leaders (Lipset & Bendix, 1959).

Education and occupational selection are the major avenues for upward mobility. People from the various social strata often have differing attitudes toward education and jobs. Thus, a national survey conducted in the 1940's showed that members of the working class, in comparison to people from higher social levels, tended to place less emphasis on the value of a college education and, in choosing an occupation, placed greater stress on factors which probably would impede upward mobility, such as job security (Hyman, 1953).

Consistent with such differences, Midwestern high school students from a background of high social status were observed to have higher educational aspirations than students from lower-level families, even when intelligence was held constant (Sewell, Haller, & Straus, 1957). Among the male students in this study, furthermore, those whose families had high social status generally had the highest occupational aspirations. Similarly, another investigation has demonstrated that boys and girls from families high in socioeconomic status typically possessed more favorable attitudes toward education than children from lower-class backgrounds (Hieronymus, 1951). In our society, then, working-class people are less prone than their middle-class peers to encourage prolonged education and risk-taking in occupational selection.

Why should a person seek out a college education or a particular form of work? One reason has to do with the individual's economic circumstances or the nature of his abilities; if his intellectual shortcomings or inadequate financial resources leave him little hope for a high-status career, he may adjust his aspirations to reality. However, in some cases a decision to go to college or to embark on a particular career is shaped by personality. As we have already seen, the strength of an individual's needs for achievement can determine his choice of occupation; boys with a high level of achievement motivation often prefer moderately difficult occupations.

But other factors are involved here as well. High-status occupations frequently require a college education and long periods of training or apprenticeship. The boy who would enter such occupations has to be able to defer gratification. He has to study or put up with arduous preliminary tasks without being able to earn much money for a considerable period. In addition, he has to be willing to undertake at least moderate risks; his sacrifices and deferred gratifications may prove to be of no avail if for one reason or another he does not enter his chosen line of work or if it turns out to be unsatisfactory. Evidence reported earlier indicates that strong needs for achievement accompany both the ability to postpone one's pleasures in the interests of larger future rewards (Mischel, 1961a) and the capacity to undertake at least moderate risks (Atkinson, 1958).

Deferred gratification and social mobility. Social scientists have long recognized the importance of deferred gratifications in entrepreneurial activity and social mobility (cf. Miller & Swanson, 1958). Two studies of adolescents provide further documentation. In the first of these (Douvan & Adelson, 1958), teenage boys representative of American youngsters of their age were divided into those who had upward, downward, or no-mobility aspirations for status, that is to say, whether their occupational hopes were higher, lower, or at the same level as their fathers' jobs. On the whole, there were no differences in social status between these three groups of boys, but the upward-aspiring youngsters appeared to be more achievement-oriented than the downward-mobile boys. The former were more likely than the latter to think a job attractive because it was "interesting" or because it might lead to success and were less inclined to emphasize the security of the job or the ease with which it could be obtained. More relevant to the present discussion, the upward-mobile boys also indicated a greater willingness to forego immediate gratification in the interests of long-range goals. They were more likely to be saving their money, usually for education or other long-term goals.

In a more recent investigation, Straus (1962) constructed a series of scales dealing with the deferment of various adolescent needs. He found that male Wisconsin high school students who seemed to show relatively strong abilities to defer the gratification of needs for affiliation, aggression, and consumption tended to have the highest academic achievement and the highest occupational aspirations, especially when they came from the middle socioeconomic stratum. People who want to climb the social ladder must be able to postpone their pleasures in the interests of their long-range goals.

Values and social mobility. Particular values may also be important for social mobility. Rosen (1959) has suggested that achievement motivation is translated into social mobility through the medium of "achievement values," values which focus the person's attention on the means toward improvement of status. Modifying a scheme previously formulated by Florence Kluckhohn, Rosen listed three basic achievement values: (1) preference for activity, maintaining the possibility of manipulating one's environment to advantage, rather than passivity; (2) preference for an individualistic, rather than a collectivistic, orientation, so that the person feels free to break his ties with his family and other primary groups and does not subordinate his needs to the wishes of these groups; and (3) preference for planning for the future and for deferring present pleasures, rather than encouraging living for the moment. He showed that New England mothers from ethnic groups having high upward-mobility rates (white Protestants, Jews, and Greeks) were more likely to possess these achievement values than mothers from groups characteristically low in upward mobility (Italians and French-Canadians). Although the achievement values varied directly with social class in this study, the differences between ethnic groups remained significant even when social status was controlled. The high-mobility ethnic groups also had higher educational aspirations for their sons when social class was held constant.

Consistent with Rosen's results, other findings also indicate that social mobility is associated with a relatively great willingness to leave family and home (McClelland, 1961, p. 318; Strodtbeck, 1957), a comparatively strong feeling of independence from the family (Douvan & Adelson, 1958), and perhaps even some felt dissatisfaction with life in one's family (Dynes, Clarke, & Dinitz, 1956). People who attain a higher social status than that possessed by their parents may well have an activistic, individualistic, and future-oriented set of values.

Whether or not such achievement values are necessary in order to steer the achievement drive toward high status, the beliefs described by Rosen are often held by people with strong achievement needs. As a consequence, it is not surprising to find that high achievement motivation is associated with occupational mobility. Crockett (1962) reanalyzed the national survey data obtained by Veroff and his colleagues in order to determine whether there was a relation between the strength of the achievement motive and status movement (defined occupationally). Only in the case of the people reared in the lower social strata did he find that those men whose occupational level was now higher than their fathers' (at the time the respondents were young) generally had higher achievement scores on the TAT than the men who had not moved upward. Achievement needs may have propelled the former group toward higher occupational levels.

Interestingly enough, and consistent with the Miller and Swanson (1958) analysis of factors making for success in a bureaucratic society, affiliation motivation was more strongly associated with upward mobility than was achievement motivation in the men who had grown up in upper-middle families. As Crockett suggested, large-scale bureaucratic organizations, in which these latter people presumably were generally employed, tend to reward cooperative and harmonious relationships. Affiliation-oriented men probably promote such congenial relationships more often than men with strong achievement needs. The latter may be too businesslike and serious in their striving for success.

Why, some people might ask, should people be concerned with moving up the social ladder? Following the line promulgated by Arnold Green (1946) and others, they contend that the middle-class individual is often torn by anxieties, insecurities, and neuroses. If he wants to be *really* happy and obtain the *really* important values of life, they argue, let the working-class person look no further than his hearth and home.

There is little empirical justification for this variation on the romantic dream of the "noble savage" who does not pursue the supposedly "false" goals of an "artificial" society. Carefully collected data indicate that high school youths tend to have more neurotic symptoms the lower their social status (Sewell, 1961) and that people in the lowest social strata have the highest rate of psychosis (Hollingshead, 1958). The typical working-class individual is probably not so happy as some casual observers have believed. Lacking money, attractive material possessions, and economic security, he undoubtedly is subjected to a good many serious frustrations.

Parental influence. We now come to the crucial question of how the child should be reared if he is to have a high level of achievement motivation. How should parents act toward their sons if they want the boys to care about doing well? Parents obviously have a considerable influence in fostering achievement motivation; the cultural, religious, and social-class conditions affecting achievement motivation frequently operate by shaping the attitudes and values that parents teach their children and by governing the ways in which mothers and fathers behave toward them.

This is not to say that parents are the sole determiners of the child's motivations. For example, although lower- and middle-class boys aspiring to high-level occupations are often encouraged in these aspirations by their parents, the boys are evidently also influenced by their friends (Simpson, 1962). Or consider the individual's willingness to undertake risks, an important element of achievement motivation, probably influenced by the frequency with which the individual has met success in the past. A working-class boy growing up under economically precarious conditions and exposed to relatively frequent frustrations because of his family's financial circumstances may well be less inclined to take chances; he has met failure too often because of factors beyond his or his family's control (cf. Hyman, 1953).

Nevertheless, it is apparently not enough to just gratify the child's wishes if he is to acquire a high level of achievement motivation. His parents must take an active role in his training by (1) establishing high standards of performance for him and (2) encouraging him to believe that he can attain these standards through his own activity.

The first investigation of child-rearing practices associated with strong achievement needs in boys (Winterbottom; cited in McClelland, 1961, pp. 340–342) suggested that training in independence is the crucial factor in the development of this motive. When women were asked to describe the expectations they had for their sons, the mothers of the boys with high achievement scores indicated that they had wanted their sons to be independent in certain activities at a comparatively early age. These activities, we should note, involved *independent mastery* (e.g., leading other children and asserting himself in children's groups, making his own friends among children his own age, trying difficult things for himself without asking for help) rather than *caretaking* (e.g., undressing and going to bed by himself). Subsequent research, however, demonstrated that it is the parents' emphasis on achievement and not independence alone that seems to be related to strong achievement motivation in their young sons (Child, Storm, & Veroff; cited in McClelland, 1961, pp. 342 f.; Krebs, 1958).

Instead of asking parents how they treated their children, Rosen and D'Andrade (1959) gave boys a series of tasks to perform in their homes and observed how their mothers and fathers interacted with them while they worked. The investigators assumed that the parents' behavior in this situation was fairly representative of how they generally acted toward their sons. Observations of the parents' behavior showed the importance of parental standards. The mothers and fathers of the boys with strong needs for achievement (as measured independently) typically set for their sons higher standards of excellence than did the other parents. As McClelland (1961, p. 351) has commented, parental indulgence or carelessness can apparently produce weak achievement needs in boys.

In addition to setting standards, the parents, especially the mothers, of the children with high achievement scores indicated that they approved of good performance by hugging and kissing their sons when they did well. They were also more likely than the parents of the low-achievement boys to exhibit warmth toward their sons while the boys worked. (Winterbottom's earlier study had also found greater warmth and greater emotional involvement in good performance in the mothers of boys with strong needs for achievement [McClelland, 1961, pp. 352 f.].) The maternal affection may have facilitated the sons' adoption of the mothers' and fathers' high standards of excellence.

Urging and encouraging a boy to do well does not mean, however, that parents should exert excessive domination and control over their sons' actions. Generalizing from a variety of findings, McClelland contended that extreme demands placed on the child—for example, expecting him to do well on a certain task when he is actually too young to cope with it —may lead to a low level of achievement motivation. Excessive parental demands may constitute too great a restrictiveness, authoritarianism, or even parental rejection (p. 345). Thus, interviews with German women noted that the mothers of boys with weak needs for achievement tended to place great value on obedience, cleanliness, politeness, and niceness (pp. 354 f.). Whatever achievement aspirations the boys had were probably stifled by their parents' extreme and frustrating insistence on compliance to their wishes.

Strong control over the boy by the father seems to be especially inhibiting as far as achievement motivation is concerned. Rosen and D'Andrade (1959) found that the highly involved mothers of the youngsters with strong needs for achievement were generally more "pushing" and dominating than the mothers of the "low" boys. These women insisted on their sons' doing well, but they nevertheless did not make the boys see themselves as incompetent and powerless. A boy did not feel cowed, apparently, as long as the domination did not come from his same-sex parent, his father. When parents and son were asked to agree on what level of performance the boy should achieve on a certain task, the fathers of the high-achievement boys stated the decision less often than the other fathers. The former were much less dominating on the whole, and the investigators concluded that high achievement motivation does not develop unless the father gives his son a good deal of autonomy so that the boy can test himself freely and gain confidence in his own skill at his own pace. Other investigations also point to the inhibiting effects of strong paternal authority. For one, Rosen (1962) attributed the comparatively low level of achievement motivation in Brazilian boys, in part at least, to the typical Brazilian father-controlled, authoritarian family. Similarly, father-dominance is said to be the reason for the relatively weak needs for achievement in the American upper class and also in Turkey (McClelland, 1961, pp. 404–406). Extreme father-dominance casts a shadow over a boy —one which inhibits the growth of his desires for independent achievement.

Conclusions. Although maternal warmth and the lack of excessive paternal control can probably be regarded as need-gratifying to the boys, the total pattern of findings described above clearly demonstrates that need-gratification does not in itself lead to strong achievement motives. It is not enough for the parent to avoid frustrating his child and to encourage him to be independent. As Rosen and D'Andrade have suggested, the parent also has to teach his son to want to do well at the tasks he undertakes. The mother and father must play an active role in inculcating these standards of excellence.

Not only is need-gratification insufficient for the development of strong achievement motivation, but continued easy satisfaction of desires may actually destroy this instigation. It is true that the evidence on this point is far from certain. Nevertheless, a number of the considerations described above are suggestive. Remember that the person with strong achievement desires generally prefers to work on moderately difficult tasks. He tends to seek out the "optimal challenge," presumably because it is only through succeeding on a challenging, moderately risky task which tests his skill and ability that he can obtain the satisfaction of a job well done. If life is always too easy for him, he will not obtain enough of these satisfactions, and his achievement motivation may weaken and die out altogether. Our society has witnessed many alterations in family fortunes, and we often hear of a family going from "shirtsleeves to shirtsleeves" in three or four generations. It may be that the father who had pulled himself up the social ladder by hard work and his striving for achievement then pampered his sons excessively. His children, having it too easy, did not themselves develop strong achievement motivation.

The "optimal challenge" requires occasional frustrations. If a task is to be sufficiently challenging, the person obviously must have some hope of doing well. But he also must know that there is some chance he will fail, and he must have experienced occasional thwartings in the past if he is to believe that there really is some risk to the undertaking. Contrary to the theorists who believe in self-actualization, we may not be helping a person in the long run if we satisfy his every whim so that he never meets failures and frustrations.

3

MORAL DEVELOPMENT

Moral Values and Judgments

Chapter 2 made reference to both "motivation" and "values."
A person with strong achievement *motivation* seeks to do
well, whereas those people with achievement *values* are presumably in favor of certain kinds of behavior, such as postponing pleasures, which are deemed necessary in order to
achieve the goal. The concept, "value," involves a person's
evaluations of particular classes of behavior, and we shall
stick to this definition in this chapter. Moral values, thus, are
evaluations of actions generally believed by the members of a
given society to be either "right" or "wrong." In more usual
terms, we can say that a person has strong moral values if he
shares in the cultural consensus; he agrees with most of the
other people in his society as to whether certain acts are
"right" or "wrong."

Such a conception has at least one major advantage. By
emphasizing the cognitive nature of values, we explicitly dis-

tinguish between evaluations and action patterns. Holding a particular belief does not necessarily imply behavior consistent with the belief; a boy may be convinced it is wrong to cheat on examinations and still cheat on an important test when he is sufficiently afraid of failure.

In this chapter, we will deal with the development and operation of moral values. The chapter begins with an examination of some of the determinants of moral judgment. Here we ask, What factors govern the individual's judgments of ethical situations, determining whether he sees a particular action as right or wrong? If a person believes some behavior is ethically improper, we ask what punishment—if any—he believes to be warranted? Next, we take moral values as socially given and discuss the formation of a strong conscience. Why does one person have strong moral values, whereas another does not? Moral behavior has to do, however, with more than just judgments and conscience. People do at times deviate from their own moral codes. They act in ways that they know (at other times) to be wrong. Why do such temporary transgressions occur? In attempting to deal with this question, the chapter concludes with an analysis of some of the conditions governing resistance to temptations.

Development of Moral Judgments

Piaget's analysis. The eminent Swiss psychologist, Jean Piaget (1948) has provided what is undoubtedly the most famous description of the development of moral judgment in children. Explicitly recognizing that they were investigating judgments and not behavior, Piaget and his collaborators questioned children "from the poorer parts of Geneva" about certain problematical situations. The children's answers sug-

gested to Piaget that there were two major stages in the formation of moral judgments: the first of these, lasting until seven
or eight years of age, involves "the morality of constraint"; the
second stage is "the morality of cooperation."

In the first stage, supposedly because the child regards
adults as dominant and omnipotent, eternal and unchanging
rules (which the child believes are handed down by adults) are
to be accepted automatically and without question. Children
also evaluate behavior in terms of objective consequences,
following what Piaget called "the principle of moral realism."
As an illustration of this important principle, consider two
(paraphrased) hypothetical situations employed by the investigators.

(1) A little boy, John, is called to dinner. Unknown to John,
behind the door to the dining room is a chair on which is a tray
holding fifteen cups. As he enters the room, the door knocks
against the tray, and all the cups are broken. (2) One day, a
little boy named Henry tried to get some jam out of a cupboard
when his mother was away from the house. He climbed on a
chair, but he could not reach it. While he was trying, however,
he knocked over a cup, which broke.

Using moral realism, the younger Swiss children indicated
that John was naughtier than Henry. He had broken fifteen
cups, whereas Henry had broken only one.

Justice is often thought at this age to be "immanent," automatically emanating from the objects in the situation. Thus,
when hearing of a little child who, contrary to his teacher's
orders, had tried to sharpen his pencil with a knife and had
cut himself, the youngsters thought that the cut was a punishment arising from the knife itself. They believed that the child
would not have cut himself if he had been allowed to use the
knife. If punishment has to be administered, it is an expiation.
The evildoer must be made to realize the seriousness of his
wicked action. The more severe the punishment, then, the

better or fairer it is. For example, according to Piaget, when a young child is told of a boy who broke a toy belonging to his little brother, he is likely to advocate expiatory punishment. Given a variety of punishments which might be administered, the youngster typically says that the boy should not be allowed to play with his own toys for a week.

The more mature type of morality, "the morality of cooperation, or reciprocity," generally begins around nine or ten years of age. The child's unilateral respect for the dominant, omnipotent adult has given way to mutual respect, cooperation, and increased autonomy for the child. Presumably as a consequence of this change, rules are now no longer regarded as fixed, externally imposed laws. The child now realizes that rules can be altered; they are not coercive, but are based on cooperation and mutual respect. His evaluations of other people's behavior reflects this change, and he considers intention ("subjective responsibility"), rather than objective consequence.

This change can be seen in the responses to the stories about the broken cups. Henry is now labeled the naughtier boy because he had intended to commit a "bad" act. Furthermore, instead of advocating retributive justice, the now-autonomous child, thinking in terms of equality, supposedly believes that punishment should follow the principle of reciprocity. Punishment should put things right, or restore the *status quo ante;* inflicting pain in retribution is not necessary. Thus, on hearing the story of the boy who had broken his little brother's toy, the older children typically called for either reciprocation—the boy should give the brother one of his own toys—or restitution —he should pay to have it mended.

According to Piaget, another type of judgment, in which there is a consideration of equity, begins to emerge at around eleven or twelve years; the child now becomes concerned with the details of the situation he is judging. Taking circumstances into account, he might now forgive certain transgressions. If he were younger, he would be more inclined to believe that the moral violation should be punished in some way merely because it is a violation. But his thought processes have changed with age, and he can now understand and forgive.

Piaget believed that the developmental sequence he described arose from a combination of environmental and maturational events. Adult constraint generally weakens as the child grows older, and much of the older child's altered way of thinking is, as we have seen, supposedly a consequence of his new-found autonomy and self-respect. But the child has also simply grown older, and his increased maturity presumably also contributes to his more sophisticated moral judgments. (We may note in this regard that European psychologists have typically made greater use of genetic or hereditary concepts in explaining human behavior than have their American counterparts. Indeed, many American writers have criticized Piaget for placing too great an emphasis on maturational determinants of moral judgments, and their criticisms appear to be justified.)

Tests of Piaget's formulation. Empirical investigations carried out in both Europe and the United States in the past thirty years or so have yielded only uneven support for Piaget's analysis. There may well be some age differences in moral judgment (Bandura & McDonald, 1963; Boehm & Nass, 1962; Bronfenbrenner, 1962), but these judgments clearly are strongly influenced by sociocultural learning. The changes that do take place with increased age are not necessarily products of an automatic maturational process. Equally important, where Piaget regarded moral judgments as forming a unitary pattern in a given developmental stage, later research indicates that there are different and independent forms of judgment even at the same age level.

In one typical investigation (Boehm & Nass, 1962), the psychologists interviewed children between six and twelve years of age using Piaget's method. Many of the youngsters below nine years, they found, displayed moral realism in response to the story of the broken cups. In contrast, the majority of the children over nine considered subjective responsibility (intent), rather than objective consequences. The older group defined naughtiness in terms of the boy's intention and not in terms of the magnitude of the damage he had created. Similarly, other research (Durkin, 1959a; Durkin, 1959b) suggests that the older the child, the greater is the consideration of equity, taking into account the circumstances of the situation being judged.

Nevertheless, the moral judgments made by older children do not always conform to Piaget's analysis. Increased age does not necessarily bring a greater advocacy of reciprocity in punishment, whether the punishment is for physical aggression (Durkin, 1959a; Durkin, 1959b) or for having violated property and personal rights (Durkin, 1959c). Contrary to Piaget's observations, older boys and girls are not always readier to insist that "it is strictly fair to give back the blows that one has received." They sometimes believe, for example, that teachers or other authorities are the appropriate people to punish a child who fights, rather than they themselves, and consequently that it is not necessary or right to give back blow for blow.

Piaget was clearly in error in maintaining that mature moral judgments inevitably entailed (1) considerations of subjective responsibility rather than moral realism; (2) a belief in reciprocal or restitutive punishment, rather than retribution; (3) an increased regard for equity; (4) a decreased belief in immanent justice; (5) rejection of the idea that punishment is more efficacious the more severe it is; *and* (6) a decreased dependence on adult authority. These components of moral thinking are not always found together (MacRae, 1954). We also know now that independence from adults in deciding what is right does not always accord with assigning blame on the basis of subjective responsibility (Boehm, 1962a).

A recent review (Bronfenbrenner, 1962) has suggested that there is less and less empirical support for the Piaget formulation the further one goes from the European mainland. Undoubtedly, as many authorities have concluded, Piaget unjustifiably minimized the influence of the child's social environment.

Cultural and class influences on moral judgments. One of the first investigations of the validity of Piaget's notions indicated that children's moral judgments are affected by both their national culture and their socioeconomic background. Noting that the Swiss psychologist had studied mostly poor children, Harrower (1934) selected a comparable sample of youngsters from the poorer parts of London and a group of children from well-to-do English homes. She found that there was a decrease in moral realism with age only in the lower-class group. The children from the more prosperous families, by contrast, tended to show relatively mature judgment even at the youngest ages (below six years), and the percentage of such evaluations remained fairly constant over the age range. Furthermore, even in the case of the lower socioeconomic groups, a higher proportion of English than Swiss children exhibited mature judgment (cf. Bronfenbrenner, 1962).

The findings obtained by this English psychologist appear to be fairly general. Other investigators have also found national and social class differences in moral judgment, and there is suggestive evidence that Swiss culture somehow tends to delay the development of mature moral evaluations—if we employ Piaget's criteria of maturity—at least in comparison to English and American society (cf. Bronfenbrenner, 1962).

Several researchers have also observed differences in moral judgment dependent on social class similar to those reported by Harrower. Thus, in one of the previously cited studies (Boehm & Nass, 1962), when they were told the stories of the broken cups, boys from the upper-middle class displayed a greater concern with the child's motivation than did the youngsters from the working class. The former said that the child was naughty if he had intended to commit the bad act. The working-class boys, on the other hand, were more likely to evaluate the deed in terms of appearance—the magnitude of the damage.

Why do we find such cultural and class differences? Bronfenbrenner (1962) has hypothesized that authoritarian and arbitrary practices of child rearing as employed by European parents, especially when dealing with their very young children, were largely responsible for the two-stage sequence observed by Piaget. The young European child was typically completely dominated by his mother and father and, thus, could have easily adopted the morality of constraint. It was not until he was older, Bronfenbrenner suggested, that he was treated in a more rational, egalitarian manner. Consistent with this reasoning, parents taking extreme points of view regarding child rearing, as is likely to be the case in authoritarian families, tend to have children who exhibit immature moral judgment, especially in the areas of immanent justice and the belief in the efficacy of extreme punishment (Johnson, 1962).

A child's experiences in a particular religious culture could conceivably also shape the exact nature of his moral evaluations. The Catholic Church, for example, regards seven years as the age of reason. A seven-year-old Catholic child must learn the difference between accidents and sinful actions so that he knows what must, and what need not, be confessed. Whether some behavior is sinful frequently depends, of course, on the intent of the action, and, consequently, young Catholic children are taught to evaluate a deed for its motivation. Not surprisingly, then, Catholic parochial school children have been found to give mature responses to Piaget-type stories at an earlier age than public school children, regardless of the social class or intelligence level of the children (Boehm, 1962b). The Catholic youngsters had learned to consider subjective responsibility because this learning was important in their religion.

Differences in learning conditions can also account for the differences in judgment displayed by middle- and working-class children. As the reader will recall, working-class youngsters are more likely than their middle-class peers to evaluate an act in terms of its consequences, rather than of its intent. This difference corresponds to differences in the major concerns of their parents. Interviews with a sample of white working-class and middle-class families in Washington, D.C. (Kohn, 1959a; Kohn, 1959b), indicated that the working-class parents gave greater attention to the surface appearances of their children's actions. They evidently wanted qualities in their children that would assure respectability. Respectability could easily be endangered or lost altogether if their children violated social prescriptions. Above all, their children had to avoid the open display of antisocial acts.

The middle-class parents, by contrast, were much more secure in their social status. They did not fear actions that would undermine a precarious social position, and they could therefore go beyond appearance. They wanted their children to develop the appropriate internal standards by which they could regulate their own behavior, and, so, they generally considered a child's motives when evaluating his behavior. There is little wonder, then, that middle-class boys and girls are also relatively prone to take subjective responsibility into account in making moral judgments. They learn to copy their parents.

the moral judgments, the child had to define "naughtiness" in terms of either objective consequences or subjective responsibility.)

In general, the researchers found, the child was most likely to have altered his initial type of evaluation when he had seen the adult being given approval for expressing these differing judgments. It mattered little whether the child had also been given approval. Furthermore, there was virtually no change in those children who had been given the social rewards without an adult being present.

The children had clearly adopted the types of judgment verbalized by the reinforced adult model. Learning experiences, especially those in which parents and other significant adults have a major role, contribute a great deal to the exact nature of the child's moral judgments. If we assume that the adequately socialized child should evaluate ethical situations in particular ways, the Bandura-McDonald findings demonstrate that it may not be enough just to gratify (reward) the child. The child will learn to make the appropriate judgments more quickly if adults actively intervene in the learning process.

The Conscience

For the layman as well as for most clinically oriented social workers, psychologists, and psychiatrists, moral behavior as well as moral judgments depend on the formation of strong consciences. The development of conscience or (to use the psychoanalytic concept) of the superego presumably eliminates the necessity of constant surveillance and threats of punishment.

When he is very young, of course, the child must be controlled by direct parental action. The mother must prevent her child from touching the hot stove or the sharp knife and keep him from wandering out into the street because he is too young to understand the dangers involved in such situations. As he gets older, he learns that his parents want him to do certain things at certain times and not to do other things. He gets approval for carrying out the desired actions and some form of punishment if he departs from his parents' standards. With time and continued learning, he comes to control himself because of his hopes of obtaining such rewards as social approval or his fears of obtaining such punishment as spanking or merely disapproval.

This type of self-control is, however, ultimately based on the anticipation of detection; the child carries out the desired action or avoids the prohibited behavior because he believes that the people who can reward or punish him will find out what he has done. It is not until he has truly internalized parental and societal moral standards that he will behave in a socially proper fashion solely because this is the "right" thing to do. He now supposedly has a strong conscience, an adequately developed superego. He can be trusted to behave in a socially appropriate manner without external threats. If he fails to act properly, he will feel guilty, and he presumably wants to avoid the arousal of guilt.

The present section examines research bearing on this common conception. Three major points are made: (1) for many people in our society, inner controls are not sufficient to inhibit socially disapproved behavior. These inner controls evidently have to be reinforced by the actions of other people. (2) The conscience should not be regarded as a unitary, everactive internal agency of the personality. (3) Parents play an active part in the development of internal standards of conduct.

External factors in moral behavior. Several anthropologists have suggested that the description of the development of conscience presented above is not applicable to all societies. In some societies, they maintain, adults act in a socially proper fashion in order to avoid shame rather than guilt. Thus, pre-World War II Japan has been characterized as a "shame," rather than a "guilt," culture (Benedict, 1946). The young Japanese, particularly the boy, supposedly developed a strong fear of ridicule in his early years and, consequently, leaned over backward to be proper in the eyes of others. He had to conform to the obligations of his role in society and preserve his reputation or he would suffer the sharp wounds of shame. (We might note, however, that this thesis has recently been questioned on the basis of projective test data [cf. Hsu, 1961, pp. 26 f.].) In a somewhat similar vein, Whiting (1959) has argued that beliefs in sorcery and witchcraft operate to control crime in primitive cultures lacking formal judicial systems. In all these societies, people supposedly inhibit their antisocial desires primarily because of fear of external events, of ridicule by others, or of punishment by magic. By contrast, our society —ideally, at least—seeks to develop strong inner controls in its members so that they can police their own actions without the threat of externally imposed sanctions.

Contrary to this ideal, however, research findings indicate that external conditions often influence the extent to which people in our society conform to moral codes. Their moral behavior depends on more than just their internal standards.

Such an observation is not altogether surprising. We certainly would expect *children* to be responsive to situational factors; they may be too young to have developed firm moral standards of their own. Nursery-school children, for example, sometimes employ nearby adults as "external superegos." If these grownups approve of or do not punish certain actions, the youngsters may well think that these actions are not really bad after all. For instance, in one study preschoolers exhibited an increase in aggressive play when they were watched by a permissive adult, but not when the adult was absent (Siegel & Kohn, 1959). Apparently, as far as the children were concerned, the permissive adult had implicitly put her stamp of approval on the morally ambiguous aggressive behavior. Further, sixth-grade school children given a projective story-completion test depicting scenes of moral transgression also showed that they were attentive to external cues in responding to these transgressions (Aronfreed, 1961). Many of the youngsters indicated that their reactions would depend greatly on the influence or demands of others in the situation rather than exclusively on their self-evaluations and internalized standards.

It is not only children, however, who are susceptible to external influences. The moral behavior of many adults is at times also governed by events taking place in the world around them, as was shown by a study conducted at a busy street corner in Austin, Texas (Lefkowitz, Blake, & Mouton, 1955). It was found that the incidence of pedestrian violations of a traffic signal was increased when one of the experimenters violated the signal, and especially if he were a person of high status. Where only about 1 per cent of the pedestrians ordinarily crossed the street against the traffic light, this figure rose to 4 per cent when the experimenter violated the signal dressed in a low-status fashion and increased to 14 per cent when he appeared to come from the higher social levels. The reader can undoubtedly think of other examples of external influences on adult moral behavior. We all know of men away from home at, say, a convention who, in the company of fun-loving friends, do what they would never do in other circumstances.

Why do social conditions affect the frequency of moral violations? Later in this section, three reasons will be offered, but one has just been suggested. If a person is not sure whether a given action is really "correct," he can find out from the other people around. If these others approve of the behavior or perhaps even if they just do not disapprove, the action may not seem too wrong after all. Conceivably, then, the people who followed the man of high status across the street against the traffic light had temporarily judged such behavior as being not too bad.

This type of influence probably occurs fairly often. Consider aggressive mobs. The individual mob member is surrounded by people calling for violence. Their shared opinions help define aggression as being morally correct or at least not incorrect, but particularly when the individual has relatively weak moral standards (cf. Berkowitz, 1962, p. 85). Similarly, movie or television scenes depicting relatively justified aggression can temporarily weaken the audience's inhibitions against aggression, perhaps because the audience's own aroused aggressive inclinations appear warranted in the light of the morally proper aggression in fantasy (Berkowitz & Rawlings, 1963). But, whatever the exact reasons for such seeming inconsistency, a youngster or an adult may indeed act immorally on a given occasion even though in other situations he knows fully that such behavior is wrong.

We must not, however, exaggerate the degree to which persons are susceptible to external influences in these respects. Some people are obviously relatively unaffected by the moral judgments of the others around them. They know that it is wrong to steal or to attack members of a disliked minority group, no matter what others may say. A Southern mob inflamed with passion may be intent on attacking Negroes, but some (if not most) of the people in the community resist the mob's moral standards. Their own sense of justice is too strong to be swayed by the opinions of those surrounding them. In general, the more convinced a person is that it is wrong to lie, steal, act aggressively, or break laws, i.e., the stronger his moral standards, then the more consistent will be his moral behavior from one situation to another. His strong moral code does not shift readily under the impact of other people's opinions.

Is there a unitary, ever-active conscience? Just as we should not think of moral behavior as being insensitive to external influences, so it is wrong to assume that a person usually possesses only one set of moral standards which is operative in all situations. The conscience is not a unitary entity ever on watch against immoral temptations. Rather, it is an abstraction referring to various ideals and behaviors, and these components may not form a consistent, ever-active whole. The person who is opposed to stealing may or may not cheat on his income tax, and he may or may not be opposed to physical force as a means of dealing with people who have insulted him.

Any number of findings contradict the assumption of a unitary, constantly operative conscience. Many people exhibit remarkably little consistency in their moral behavior from one occasion to the next (Hartshorne & May, 1928); and there are several supposedly important manifestations of a strong conscience which turn out not to be found in all people. For example, some authorities (e.g., Sears, 1960) have proposed that there are at least three related aspects of the conscience: feelings of guilt, resistance to temptation, and moral ideals. Any one of these aspects may indicate the presence of the others; a child exhibiting strong restraints against temptation would then necessarily be prone to strong guilt feelings should he ever violate his strong moral standards.

Thus, investigators have at times used signs of guilt as an index of conscience strength (e.g., Sears, Maccoby, & Levin, 1957; Whiting & Child, 1953). Guilt feelings are not, however, always correlated with resistance to temptation (cf. Hoffman, 1962). Persons who show signs of great guilt when they violate moral norms in one situation are not necessarily immune to temptations in other situations.

A study employing four-year-old middle-class children (Burton, Maccoby, & Allinsmith, 1961) is illustrative. Each child played a game in which he could win an attractive prize. After a preliminary session, the experimenter left the room, ostensibly providing the youngster with an opportunity to cheat, although the child's behavior was actually being recorded by a hidden observer. It was found that the children who did not resist the temptation typically exhibited frequent and strong guilt feelings at home (as reported by their mothers in separate interviews). They were aware of moral standards. When they did wrong at home, they were likely to feel guilty and confess their misdeeds. Yet their moral knowledge and their predisposition to strong guilt reaction following a transgression had not protected them from misdeeds.

There are also other grounds for questioning the single-conscience doctrine. The previously cited investigation also found that the child-rearing conditions that apparently produce strong restraints against immoral temptations are quite different from the training conditions that give rise to frequent guilt feelings. Then, too, there may even be different kinds of guilt; guilt about aggressive behavior and guilt over disobedience to one's parents evidently do not have the same developmental origins (Allinsmith, 1957). All in all, we have little reason to picture the conscience as a constantly alert, unitary, and internal law-enforcing agency.

One way to resolve some of the difficulties confronting the usual conception of the conscience is to recast the role of moral values. As we have seen, many authorities contend that the socialized individual avoids doing wrong in order to prevent the arousal of guilt. A person who is tempted to transgress presumably experiences an automatic anticipatory guilt reaction which comes as a signal of the strong discomfort (guilt feelings) that would arise should he succumb to the lure of the misdeed, and then he supposedly resists the temptation. Nevertheless, guilt may not arise in many people until they realize that they have violated one of their moral standards. Guilt implies possession of moral values, but these values may not be operative when the temptation occurs.

A schoolboy may look at his neighbor's test paper during an important examination without thinking that such cheating is wrong. He might be so preoccupied with passing the test that he does not become aware that he has done anything wrong until later. Or—as apparently happened in the case of the people who followed the experimenter across the street against the traffic light—other factors in the situation may alter the individual's judgment of what is proper. The schoolboy's evaluation of his own behavior during the examination could well be influenced by the behavior or opinions of his classmates. He might think that cheating is proper if he sees many of his peers cheat or if they had agreed beforehand that everyone had to help everyone else. Similarly, his judgment could be distorted momentarily under the press of strong desires; he might be so afraid of failing the test that he just does not think of his disapproval of cheating. At any rate, whatever the circumstances, the boy does not think of himself at the time as doing something wrong. He does not become aware of the significance of his action until later, and only then does he feel the twinges of guilt.

Let us carry this analysis one step further. Suppose that this youngster did have a guilt reaction later; what could he do? One possibility, of course, would be to berate himself or to confess his misdeed to someone else. The burden of guilt might then have been lifted from his shoulders. He would have received his punishment—from himself or from the other person —and his transgression would be "paid for." The punishment alleviates his guilt (Bandura & Walters, 1963). Rather than signifying a strong conscience, confession or self-beratement in some instances may be only a learned way of reducing guilt —guilt which never would have arisen had the moral values been initially stronger.

We know from the boy's behavior in this case that he is capable of strong guilt feelings. Such a reaction only indicates, however, that he knows that it is wrong to cheat and that he has departed from his own code of conduct; he does possess a moral value against cheating. This value becomes stronger as he learns to regard any form of cheating as a departure from the standards he holds for himself. It is thus that he learns to apply the value more and more often in a wider range of situations. The scope of his conscience increases.

But the reader should also remember that all we definitely know about this boy is that he has a value against cheating. We are not certain that he thinks it wrong to hit girls or that he believes that he should help people who are dependent on him. There is a fairly good probability that he will possess a wide variety of moral standards, but such standards are the product of his learning experiences. Consistent, far-ranging moral values arise from the consistency and breadth of his learning, and not from any such unified internal entity as a single conscience.

With this warning against the notion of an ever-active, unified moral agency in man, let us proceed to a consideration of some social and familial influences on the development of moral values. The present discussion will focus on the development of moral values in boys. Most of the research in this area has dealt only with boys, and we cannot be certain that the development of conscience in girls follows the same principles. If we occasionally use the phrase "strong conscience" in this discussion, it will not imply a single entity. To say that a middle-class person has a "strong conscience" means (among other things) that he has a relatively great number of strongly impressed and comparatively stable moral values.

Development of Conscience

Religious influences on moral standards. American political and religious leaders often say that our society rests ultimately on religion. Such a statement implies at the least that religion contributes to social order. Without religion, there presumably would be an increase in violence, crime, and corruption. Undoubtedly, this view is widely held. A recent magazine article told of a panel of citizens which had the power to decide which of many applicants could benefit from a life-saving machine that could cleanse their diseased kidneys. Religious activity apparently was one of the criteria the panel employed in making the selections: did the applicant belong to an organized religious group and attend services? A religious person supposedly was a better member of society than one who was not.

Statistical data, however, cast some doubt on the importance of religious participation. The man who attends church may be more law-abiding than the man who does not, although this is far from certain, but there is little evidence that the church member's religious training has influenced his moral behavior, or at least the kind of behavior with which the medical panel was likely to be concerned.

Some of the findings in the classic "Studies in Deceit" conducted by Hartshorne and May (1928) are pertinent here. These investigators presented a large battery of deception tests to thousands of children from eight to sixteen years of age and observed whether each child cheated or otherwise acted in a dishonest fashion in the tests. Those youngsters who were enrolled in Sunday schools, they found, generally were more honest than the children who did not go to Sunday school. Undoubtedly, however, a factor of selection was operating here. Most likely, the children who were placed in Sunday schools by their parents had stronger moral standards to begin with, at least with regard to honesty. Church attendance in itself did not seem to lead to increased honesty; the frequency of Sunday school attendance showed no correlation with the amount of honesty displayed by the children.

Among other things, we have to recognize that there are various kinds of religious belief and various kinds of moral behavior. Illustrating the necessity of distinguishing among the various forms of religious belief, a substantial body of research indicates that "religious" people tend to be more prejudiced against Negroes and Jews than are those who are not "religious." It may be that ethnic bias is really characteristic only of those who are religious for utilitarian, self-serving purposes and that it is much less common in people who have a strong, purely personal involvement in religion (Wilson, 1960). Merely belonging to an organized church and learning conventional religious values does not necessarily mean that a person is a good citizen or is free of ethnic prejudice.

There are, moreover, various kinds of moral behavior, only some of which may be governed by religious beliefs. Two sociologists (Middleton & Putney, 1962) differentiated between antiascetic and antisocial violations of moral standards, pointing out that religious training may increase asceticism but does not necessarily affect antisocial behavior. A large sample of middle-class college students in Florida and California was given questionnaires to be filled out anonymously. Those students who described themselves as believing in a personal God reported they had engaged in fewer violations of traditional ascetic standards against gambling or nonmarital sexual intercourse than did the religious skeptics. There was, however, no over-all difference between the "believers" and the "skeptics" in the extent to which they regarded antisocial violations (such as shoplifting, cheating on exams, and striking another person in anger) as wrong. Nor was there any difference between these groups in the reported frequency of carrying out these antisocial actions.

If we can generalize from such studies—and the famous Kinsey report (Kinsey, Pomeroy, & Martin, 1948) supports the finding for religion and sexual behavior—we obviously have to change our expectations regarding the effects of religious training. Religion as it is currently practiced may promote asceticism, at least in some cases, but it does not in itself reduce the incidence of stealing, cheating, or aggression. We may still want to give our young people religious training, but that would be for other reasons. We cannot expect religious training as it is ordinarily provided to lessen antisocial immorality.

Social-class influences on morality. Many people from the lower social strata do not possess the values characteristic of middle-class culture. Such class differences exist for moral as well as achievement values. Thus, presumably because they have differing sexual standards, American working-class men typically have a higher frequency of sexual intercourse than do middle-class males (Kinsey et al., 1948). Moreover, the lower-class individual is also more likely to engage in antisocial behavior.

Sociologists have long emphasized the contribution of social class, neighborhood, and community to criminality and delinquency. Gangland in Chicago, for example, is concentrated in a social-twilight zone of factories, deteriorated housing, poverty, and cultural change. These deteriorated, poverty-stricken areas, inhabited by members of the working class, have high delinquency and crime rates. Similar statistics can be reported from practically every city on the globe. The statistics are more definite, however, than the reasons for them. Although the evidence is not so good as we would want, there appear to be at least three connected reasons for the high rates of crime at the lowest social levels: (1) frequent economic and social frustrations leading to antisocial aggressive behavior (Berkowitz, 1962); (2) class-engendered conditions interfering with the development of conventional moral standards; and (3) parental treatment.

Criminal and deviant behavior sometimes arises as a rebellion against middle-class agencies and moral standards. The eminent sociologist Robert Merton has maintained (1957) that deviant behavior is frequently the product of an "acute disjunction" between culturally prescribed goals and institutionalized means for attaining these goals. Putting this more simply, he contended that regulatory social norms break down, traditional rules lose their authority, when a person is denied the means to the satisfaction of his wishes. Albert K. Cohen (1955) has extended this reasoning to the formation of delinquent cultures in juvenile gangs. He views a good deal of juvenile delinquency as stemming from deprivations in status. Growing up in a society dominated by middle-class attitudes and aspirations, the working-class child is taught that ambition, hard work, self-control, respect for property, and the postponement of gratifications lead to academic success, financial achievement, and the rewards of high social status. He soon learns, however, that he has little real chance to escape from his working-class environment. The background of his social class does not equip him to meet the terms of success established by middle-class institutions, and he experiences a serious deprivation in status together with a decline in self-esteem. The result is supposedly a "reaction formation." He repudiates middle-class norms and substitutes "nonutilitarian, malicious, and negativistic" values.

Frustrations in respect of status are not solely responsible for antisocial behavior, however. For most delinquents and criminals, it is apparently not enough just to say that they have experienced severe thwartings. They have had to learn criminal techniques, and, more than this, their aggressive, antisocial inclinations generally have had to be supported by the values of their friends and peers. Several criminologists have pointed out that delinquents adopt the attitudes and behavior patterns of their associates. Sharing similar values, the youngsters convince one another that their antisocial actions are "right." They develop a delinquent subculture that defines in its own terms what behavior is proper and what improper. The boy who would gain acceptance or maintain his membership in such a society must act as the others do, and, being attracted to the gang, he is likely to regard the gang values as "correct."

Shared group attitudes are undoubtedly important in the control of hostile urges engendered by social and personal frustrations. These attitudes, forming part of the culture of the group (or community or region), prescribe and justify given actions in particular situations. They may maintain that an offended person should "turn the other cheek," or they may insist that he should strike back at his tormenter in order to redeem his honor. Regional and community differences in homicides and other crimes probably are due, in part at least, to differences in such shared values. Thus, the South Atlantic states had more than six times as many homicides per 100,000 in population as did the New England states in 1958, perhaps because the social code of the lower-class Southerner often says that he must seek personal retribution for any "wrongs" done him. He may have been exposed to more serious economic thwartings than his New England counterpart because of the greater poverty of his part of the country, but his social code also permits him to reveal what anger he may feel and may even call for personal violence in some situations. As several authorities have suggested (cf. Berkowitz, 1962, pp. 320 f.), many murders take place in a subculture of violence which gives social approval to quick resort to physical aggression.

Shared values can also account for urban-rural differences in the relation between social class and delinquency. According to one study (Clark & Wenninger, 1962) conducted with adolescent school children in various communities, youngsters from working-class backgrounds who resided in rural or small-town areas did not admit committing more illegal actions than did the higher-class children from these areas. However, there was a difference between the social classes in admitted illegal behavior for the school children living in a large metropolitan center or in areas containing one dominant social class. The most serious offenses were generally committed by lower-class urban youngsters. The shared values of their community probably encouraged and justified, or at least did not strongly condemn, illegal behavior.

Again we must note that criminality is not due to one set of factors, that criminal associations are not the sole causes of antisocial behavior. I have argued elsewhere (Berkowitz, 1962, pp. 314 f.) that a person may associate with lawbreakers and accept their values because he has a history of prior frustrations. Friendships and gang memberships do not arise entirely by chance. Crowded city streets frequently provide boys and girls with a wide variety of possible friends, and they can and do exert some selection.

There is evidence of such a selection of friends in the well-known comparison of delinquent and nondelinquent boys published by Sheldon and Eleanor Glueck (1950). Even though the youngsters in this study were fairly similar demographically, a much smaller proportion of the nondelinquents had persistent lawbreakers as friends. These children seem to have avoided all but the most superficial contact with their delinquent peers. In contrast, many of the youthful offenders appear to have gone out of their way to look for antisocial companions. More frequently than the "normal" children, the delinquents played in neighborhoods relatively far from home and sought out older boys as companions. Their gang membership could have had an important part in strengthening their aggressive tendencies and in weakening their restraints against socially disapproved behavior, but their friendships had not always come about fortuitously. The delinquents could well have selected aggressively antisocial youngsters as friends because of their own hostile desires.

Selective factors also operate in the acquisition of values and attitudes. Social-psychological research has demonstrated again and again that people do not automatically adopt whatever views their peers happen to advocate. Some attitudes are accepted, and others are resisted. In general, we take over most readily those beliefs and values which are consistent with our own initial inclinations. We may not assimilate another's hostile values, for example, unless we ourselves have strong aggressive tendencies. As an illustration, in one laboratory experiment (Weiss & Fine, 1956; cited in Berkowitz, 1962, p. 314) it was shown that college students accepted the aggressive beliefs expressed by a communicator when they had been angered by deliberate frustrations, but did not adopt these beliefs when they had not been provoked. A similar process is undoubtedly at work in the formation of the delinquent cultures described by Cohen and others. Young offenders reject values which are inconsistent with their aggressive desires and readily adopt other values which support such desires and permit them free expression. Their attitudes are not like clay to be shaped easily and quickly by the people with whom they happen to associate, especially by the time they reach adolescence.

Parental influence. A child's home life plays a major role in his choice of friends. If his family is bound together by ties of affection, it becomes a "bulwark against antisocial influences . . . from the neighborhood or the peer group" (Toby, 1957; cited in Berkowitz, 1962, p. 315; cf. also Brown, Morrison, & Couch, 1947). Family cohesiveness counters delinquent neighborhood and peer influences in at least three ways. For one, home life can determine the extent to which the boy becomes attracted to aggressively antisocial activities outside the home. Those youngsters not exposed to frequent severe frustrations in their families probably do not have strong aggressive urges, and so they are not drawn to groups encouraging the expression of hostility. Nor are they overinterested in obtaining adventurous (if not reckless) outlets for their emotional tensions. Delinquent activities have comparatively little attraction for them.

In addition, a secure, emotionally satisfying family life probably facilitates the development of law-abiding self-concepts. Seeing himself in a certain way, the youngster cannot readily conceive of himself as engaging in unlawful activities. Delinquent behavior does not accord with the standards he has set for himself. Consistent with this last point, one study (Reckless et al., 1957; cited in Berkowitz, 1962, p. 316) found that boys living in areas of high delinquency who were regarded by their teachers as probable nondelinquents were more likely than potential delinquents (as judged by their teachers) to have self-concepts which would presumably "insulate" them from criminal behavior. The boys' self-concepts were undoubtedly shaped in part by their parents' treatment of them.

Third, the family, especially the parents, may teach the child —implicitly or explicitly—either to engage in socially disapproved actions or to avoid such behavior. Let us examine this educational process in some detail by considering, first, the child's identification with his parents; then effects of various disciplinary practices; and, finally, the modeling influences the mother and father often exert on the youngster.

Parental Influences in Conscience-Formation

Identification. We have all seen young children trying to imitate their parents. Girls dress up in their mothers' clothes. They play with dolls and, acting as though they were the mothers, may spank the dolls or require them to hang up their clothes and put their toys away. Boys copy their fathers when they make believe that they are driving the family automobile or going off to work. But, although this imitation is most clearly revealed in children's play, it is a mistake to think that children copy their parents only in their games or that they imitate only their mothers' and fathers' formal roles. Psychoanalytic observations show that many people take over a variety of qualities from their parents—their political party preferences, their tastes in food or clothing, their beliefs, and, frequently, their moral values. Psychoanalytic theory refers to this taking-over process as "identification"; the child has supposedly molded his ego after the person he selected as his model. Since identification presumably has a major role in the development of the individual's conscience (or superego), we might well ask what conditions foster identification.

Most authorities, whether they are strict adherents to psychoanalytic theory or not, seem to view identification as a defensive process. They maintain that the child tries to become like his parent—or perhaps even attempts to *be* the parent—in order to reduce his anxiety. There are, however, two differing conceptions as to the source of the anxiety the child seeks to eliminate. One position, postulating a developmental or "anaclitic" identification process (Bronfenbrenner, 1960), contends that the youngster is afraid of losing the parents' love. Since they have been loving to him, he has developed a strong emotional tie to them and is presumably greatly concerned with keeping their love. He then strives to become like his parents so as to assure himself of their continued affection.

Several investigations have obtained findings consistent with this conception (cf. Hoffman, 1962). In one of these (Payne & Mussen, 1956), a high school boy was said to be strongly identified with his father if his scores on a personality inventory were closer to his father's than to his mother's. Since he also gave, on the average, masculine responses to a masculinity–femininity test, it does seem reasonable to assume that the boy had taken over his father's masculine role, i.e., that he had to some extent modeled himself after his father. In general, the father-identified boys described their family life as being fairly happy; but, perhaps most important, they regarded their fathers as rewarders rather than as punishers and as more rewarding than their mothers. It may have been the fathers' warmth and affection toward their sons that induced the boys to mold themselves after their fathers, perhaps because the boys believed that they could better keep their loved fathers' esteem by copying them.

Parental warmth is, however, probably not the only factor governing identification. Psychoanalytic theory maintains that the young child identifies with his same-sex parent in order to lessen his fear of being punished (more specifically, castrated) by the parent. Anna Freud (1937) has termed this process "identification with the aggressor." As is well known, the child supposedly has sexual desires toward his parent of the opposite sex during the Oedipal stage of his development, but fears his powerful parent of the same sex. Seeking to eliminate this danger, he theoretically tries to become the parent of the same sex. (It is as though the boy said to himself, "My father can't hurt me—I *am* my father.")

Although the two conceptions just presented (in highly simplified form) constitute the most frequent versions of the identification hypothesis, other formulations have been advanced in recent years. Whiting (1960) has proposed a "status-envy" analysis, suggesting that the child will attempt to emulate the person who enjoys "resources of high value to him when he [the child] is deprived" of these resources. The boy molds himself after his father supposedly because he envies his father, particularly his father's consumption of resources that the boy wants for himself and cannot get.

In contrast to this thesis, Mussen and Distler (1959) have argued that identification with a model depends on that model's power—his ability to either reward or punish the individual. As was reported (see page 5), psychologists found that boys who were strongly identified with the male role (i.e., who exhibited masculine interests on a projective test), presumably as a consequence of identification with their fathers, tended to view their fathers as powerful sources of both reward and punishment. Extending this line of thought, Mussen and his colleagues (Mussen, Conger, & Kagan, 1963, p. 263) now maintain that the child copies his parent because the parent controls goals that the child desires, such as power over the child and other people, mastery of the environment, and love. The young boy, they say, sees a discrepancy between his own and his father's ability to control such areas of pleasure, power, and mastery and, consequently, attempts to acquire the father's attributes.

Bandura, Ross, and Ross (1963) have conducted an intriguing experimental test of three conceptions of identification, employing three-person groups (consisting of male and female adults plus a child) representing prototypes of the nuclear family. In the first condition, one of the adults controlled access to resources valued by the child (attractive toys), while the other adult was the "resource consumer," who was allowed to play with these toys. The child was ignored in this condition. In a second condition, one of the adults again controlled the resources, but this time the child was the consumer, and the other adult was given the subordinate role. Following this, the two adults exhibited various kinds of behavior in the presence of the child, and the experimenter recorded the extent to which the child imitated each of them.

Now, what do we expect? According to the status-envy theory, the child should copy the adult consumer. The power theory, however, predicts that the child would imitate the adult who had control over the valued resources, the toys. The conception of identification as secondary reinforcement favored by many learning theorists suggests that the child will exhibit the greatest amount of imitation when he had been rewarded by being given the toys and that he will tend to copy the rewarding adult.

The experimental findings clearly supported the social-power theory. In both conditions, the children imitated the resource-controller most frequently, regardless of whether they or the other person had been successful in getting the toys. We might say they had identified with the powerful rather than the envied adult and that this had happened even when they had obtained no rewards from the former.

It is possible, of course, to interpret the two classic analyses of identification in terms of the power formulation, as Mussen and his co-workers have done. The child presumably takes on the qualities of the powerful adult member of his family who controls access to the resources he values, whether these resources are love, safety from danger, or mastery.

Knowledge of the conditions fostering the child's identification with his parents would probably increase our understanding of the parents' role in the growth of the child's conscience. This is not to say, however, that identification is the major aspect of moral development, as some writers have assumed. Identification is certainly not the only factor involved in the learning of values and attitudes. Nor is there any empirical evidence that the child seeks to emulate his parents *in all respects* (Hoffman, 1962). The youngster may take over his parent's political views and may want to be as skillful and powerful as his father, but still he may not adopt his father's moral standards. In general, there is much more to moral development than just identification.

Parental discipline. Even if the child does not copy his father or mother in every detail, the manner in which his parents have treated him contributes a great deal to his moral development. He is particularly likely to be influenced by the way in which his parents exert discipline.

Parental disciplinary techniques can be classified in a number of ways, but child psychologists have recently begun to emphasize a distinction, first proposed by Whiting and Child (1953), between love-oriented and non-love-oriented methods. Influenced by Freud's (1933) analysis of superego-formation, Whiting and Child suggested that the child's self-control has its roots in his fear of the loss of parental love. Guilt, then, is supposedly most likely to develop if the parents (1) make the child concerned with keeping their affection by being loving toward him and (2) at the same time make the child somewhat uncertain about his gaining their love. Thus, for Whiting and Child, optimal moral development is produced by conditional rather than "unconditional positive regard."

To test their hypothesis, they divided thirty-five primitive societies into those making relatively great use of love-oriented discipline (punishing by loss of love, threats of denial of reward, or threats of ostracism) and those making little use of such methods (emphasizing physical punishment, threats of such punishment, or threats of ridicule) and related this classification to the degree of personal guilt apparently prevalent in the societies (as indicated by beliefs that an individual was personally responsible for any illness he suffered). A significant relationship was obtained. Strong guilt feelings evidently tend to be present in those primitive groups relying heavily on love-oriented techniques of controlling their children.

Other research by Whiting and his students (cited in Bronfenbrenner, 1962) lends further cross-cultural support to the notion that love-oriented control methods facilitate the internalization of moral standards. Children in three cultures in the American Southwest—a Mormon community, a Texas town, and a Zuñi pueblo—completed a projective story-test in which they presumably indicated how they would respond to moral transgressions. The Mormon parents, it was found, were the ones who were most prone to withdraw affection in punishing their children, and Mormon children showed the greatest evidence of internalized moral standards. Furthermore, in each of the three cultures, the more the child was disciplined through withdrawal of affection, the greater was the likelihood that he had assimilated moral values.

Evidence from other American groups is consistent with the findings obtained by Whiting and his collaborators. Although much of the research distinguishes between psychological discipline and corporal punishment, there is a considerable overlap in the definitions of love-oriented and psychological techniques (cf. Sears, 1960, p. 104). Parents making extensive use of such methods (1) customarily reward their children by giving love (for example, by praising them) and (2) punish noncompliance with their wishes by threatening to withhold love (by showing that they are hurt or disappointed). Psychological discipline also involves a reliance on reasoning; when their children do something wrong, the parents try to explain to them how they have behaved incorrectly. In general, then, this kind of control focuses on subtle emotional manipulation, rather than on tangible rewards (such as giving presents) or concrete punishments (such as deprivation of privileges or spankings).

Psychologists have not always made this point explicit, but we will assume here that psychological discipline fosters development of conscience by facilitating the extent to which the child will adopt his parents' moral values. Psychological control will not in and of itself lead to morally proper behavior. The mother and father may reason with the child and try to make him feel guilty or ashamed when he does something of which they disapprove, and still the child may not grow up to have a strong conscience. The parents probably also have to demonstrate to the child that they want him to behave in a moral fashion and that they themselves act in this way. Their love and their methods of controlling the child encourage him to take over their values, to do as they do.

One of the first investigations of the possible child-rearing antecedents of moral behavior (MacKinnon, 1938) compared college students who had cheated on some difficult problems assigned to them to other students who had not cheated on these tasks. When asked to describe the way their parents had exercised discipline, a higher proportion of the cheaters reported that their fathers had made frequent use of physical punishment, rather than psychological techniques. On the other hand, the fathers' use of psychological methods of control had evidently encouraged the development of strong moral values, particularly against cheating, in the sons, and, in this situation, the values kept the students from transgression.

Sears, Maccoby, and Levin (1957) have also found that love-oriented (or psychological) techniques are associated with strong moral values in children. In this study, the development of conscience (possession of moral values) was inferred from the child's behavior after he had done something wrong; he was assumed to have a strong conscience if he characteristically confessed his misdeeds or acted as though he were greatly upset about them. The results of this investigation are especially instructive. A parent's threat to withdraw love will obviously not be overly upsetting to a child who has not learned to want this love. His love for his parents will be strongest and he will be most concerned with maintaining their love for him if they had been warm and affectionate toward him.

Consistent with this reasoning, Sears and his colleagues observed a relationship between the mother's frequent use of withdrawal-of-love methods and strong consciences in the child only for those mothers who were relatively warm toward their children. The mothers who were fairly cold toward their offspring and who threatened to withhold love in disciplining them were least likely to have children with strong moral values. The researchers' conclusion certainly appears warranted: "Withdrawing love where little exists is meaningless" (p. 388).

Psychological discipline also facilitates the growth of values impeding aggressive and antisocial behavior. Bandura and Walters (1959) interviewed two groups of parents with teen-aged boys: one group whose sons were in trouble with the law for aggressively antisocial offenses and a sociologically comparable group having more law-abiding youngsters. The parents of the antisocial boys were more likely to resort to physical punishment and deprivation of privileges in disciplining their children and made less use of reasoning in trying to get compliance with their demands. The parents did not, however, differ in the extent to which they explicitly threatened the child with loss of love, and the investigators suggested that such a disciplinary technique is relatively ineffective for achieving control of adolescents. Thus, though withdrawal of love did not seem related to moral behavior in teen-aged boys, the parents of the delinquent youngsters made greater use of material rewards and punishments than the methods of psychological control. (We might also note that the parents of the law-abiding boys were also more affectionate toward their sons than were the other mothers and fathers.)

In studies with younger children, researchers have shown that parents relying primarily on physical punishment instead of psychological disciplinary techniques tend to have children who display a good deal of overt hostility in their school groups (Hoffman, 1960) or relatively weak inhibitions against aggression in projective-test stories (Allinsmith, 1960). Corporal punishment has apparently not fostered that growth of strong values which would restrain antisocial aggression.

Social-class differences in antisocial aggression may be due in part to differences in the type of disciplinary technique employed by parents. Though there are many exceptions, working-class boys seem to be more ready to engage in overt acts of aggression than do their middle-class peers. This difference is shown, for example, in a study (Allinsmith, 1960) in which seventh- to ninth-grade boys were asked to complete stories depicting frustrating events. The working-class children indicated more frequently than those from the middle class that they would respond to the thwarting with the most direct forms of aggression—direct attacks on the instigator. Demonstrating differences between the social classes in child training, the psychologist also found that socioeconomic level influenced the form of discipline practiced by the mothers. The working-class women generally favored physical punishment as a control, whereas their middle-class counterparts were more likely to prefer psychological discipline.

Similarly, other research (Aronfreed, 1961) has noted that middle-class mothers tend to rely heavily on disciplinary techniques focused on inducing stable moral standards in their children, whereas lower-class mothers are more prone to employ methods which "merely sensitize their children to the painful external consequences of transgression," such as spanking.

Although the difference may be diminishing (Bronfenbrenner, 1958), middle-class parents are apparently more likely than parents lower in the social scale to prefer love-oriented or psychological forms of control of their children. This type of treatment evidently facilitates the development in their children of fairly stable attitudinal prohibitions against such antisocial behavior as aggression and cheating.

Physical punishment may, indeed, be more effective in controlling the antisocial actions of very young children. Observations of four-year-old nursery school children from middle-class homes (Burton, Maccoby, & Allinsmith, 1961) suggest that parental reliance on the more direct and severe physical modes of discipline tends to produce children who are somewhat resistant to temptations to cheat. Maternal use of reasoning was associated in this study with cheating by the child. It may be that, the more these very young children were disciplined with punishment in the home, the more they anticipated punishment for cheating in the laboratory situation. In a sense, they expected to get caught if they transgressed. They were too young to realize that they might "get away with it" in the laboratory.

Why does psychological discipline foster the growth of strong moral values? Several reasons can again be suggested. To begin with, punishment is a relatively inefficient means of exerting control (cf. Berkowitz, 1962, pp. 288 f.). As a frustration, it engenders hostility in the person who is punished, and he may reject the values of his disliked tormenter. If he does accede to the wishes of the punishing agent, it is only because of his fear. The child will do what the punitive parents demand only as long as he thinks that they will find out about his actions; he may not follow their prescriptions at all if he thinks he can "get away with it." The parent relying heavily on punishment must be continually on guard, because his child is likely to rebel against his wishes.

Not only is punishment essentially negative, but love-oriented methods may cause the child to *want* to do what his parents call for. The mothers and fathers who employ psychological control methods are typically warm and affectionate toward their children (Sears et al., 1957; Bandura & Walters, 1959). They have taught their children to love them and to desire their love in return and then have made the gaining of this love contingent on complying with their wishes. In other words, they have fostered those conditions in which their children are most likely to want to take over their values. If these parents insist on moral, socially responsible behavior, their children are motivated to comply with their wishes.

Modeling influences. Parents teach their children how to act in certain situations by the examples they provide for their offspring as well as by their explicit commands and prescriptions. Parental discipline can also shape a child's behavior, then, through modeling effects. When a father or mother spanks a child, the youngster is given an aggressive model to copy (Sears et al., 1957). Similarly, if a child's parents try to control him through appeals to reason and guilt, they serve as nonaggressive examples for him.

Modeling influences are extremely widespread, especially in our small, nuclear families. Bandura and Walters (1959) found in their survey, for instance, that the fathers of the aggressively antisocial teenagers could have been aggressive models for the boys, since these men tended to be fairly hostile and punitive themselves. Later, Bandura (cited in Berkowitz, 1962, p. 296) compared the parental treatment given to a sample of aggressive but nondelinquent youngsters to that given to a demographically similar but nonaggressive group of boys. There was no evidence that the aggressive boys had experienced greater frustrations. Their frequent hostility expressed in school and on the playground was evidently not a reaction to severe emotional thwartings in the home. Instead, the difference between the two groups seemed to be due mainly to modeling. The aggressive children usually had aggressive parents (who also frequently rewarded the youngsters' aggressive actions outside the home), whereas the mothers and fathers of the inhibited boys were themselves generally anxious and inhibited. The sons were chips off the parental blocks.

There is additional evidence of the effects of modeling in the previously mentioned investigation by Allinsmith (1960). The boys exhibiting relatively strong restraints against hostility on the projective test had in general emotionally controlled mothers, whereas the less inhibited boys had less controlled mothers. The mothers could have served as models for their sons even though they were of the other sex. If we go back even further to the classic studies of moral character by Hartshorne and May (1928), we find another illustration of such an influence. These investigators, in one phase of their exploration, compared the home lives of the fifty most honest and fifty least honest youngsters in one of their samples. They found that the parents of the worst offenders were usually socially bad models for their youngsters.

The findings seem clear. Parents' actions set an example for their children. If the mother and father are characteristically law-abiding and nonaggressive, there is a good chance that their children will also behave in a similarly moral and socially responsible fashion. On the other hand, parents may have only themselves to blame if their sons and daughters display frequent immorality and aggressiveness in their daily lives; to some extent, at least, the children are likely to be emulating their elders.

There are limitations, of course, to the effects of modeling. Just as children do not automatically adopt the attitudes and values of the people with whom they associate, so they will not necessarily model themselves after their parents. Some parents may induce their children to imitate them to a greater extent than do others. As we saw earlier, children are especially likely to copy those adults who command access to desirable goals and resources. Thus, a boy may fail to copy his father to any great degree if his mother and not his father is the kingpin of the family, the one who provides both love and security, or if his father is absent from the scene (cf. Berkowitz, 1962, pp. 296 f.).

Cultural pressures can also impose restrictions on modeling. Some sorts of action, for example, are typically appropriate for one sex but not the other. Girls are taught that they should not fight, even though their brothers are encouraged to display overt aggression (as when they are attacked by other boys). Girls learn that direct, overt aggression is not ladylike. Thus, according to research by Bandura and his students (cited in Berkowitz, 1962, p. 298), girls may be reluctant to imitate an adult's aggressive actions even when the adult is a woman. They know that direct aggression is not consistent with their sex role.

Despite such limitations, there can be little question that parents and other adults do, indeed, shape children's actions by the examples they provide. Youngsters are molded by significant adults in a variety of ways, both obvious and subtle. Their parents play an active role in the development of their moral characters by gratifying their needs, by teaching standards of conduct, and by serving as models. Contrary to the views promulgated by the theorists of self-actualization, we certainly have no evidence that a child will necessarily grow up to be a moral, responsible citizen, even though he be never frustrated, without the intervening influence of such modeling.

Parental consistency. The consistency with which mothers and fathers impose standards on their offspring may be even more important than the exact manner in which these standards are enforced. Observers have often noted the absence of firm, consistent behavioral standards in the home lives of delinquent or aggressively antisocial youngsters (Glueck & Glueck, 1950). Bandura and Walters (1959) found that the parents of their "normal" children, particularly the mothers, imposed stronger restrictions and demands on their sons than did the parents of the hyperaggressive adolescents and were also more consistent in their discipline. Moreover, despite their relative freedom from parental control, the habitually hostile youngsters were much more inclined to resent whatever demands their parents did make.

Inconsistent prescriptions for behavior can be frustrating, at least to some extent; the child faced by shifting standards does not know what to expect. Not having anticipated a parental demand or restriction, he may become angry and rebellious when told to do things he does not want to do, for people are more disturbed by unexpected than by expected thwartings of their desires. Furthermore, vacillating parental rules cannot become the basis of firm moral values. How certain can a child be that lying is wrong if his parents punish him for lying on one occasion and then shrug off another of his falsehoods at another time? The youngster could conclude with reason that lying is not so bad after all. Similarly, he could come to feel that cheating and acting aggressively are not really wrong if his parents frown on such behavior in one situation and then seemingly approve it at other times. There is some evidence that many American children exhibit a greater degree of consistency in the realm of cheating than in most other forms of moral behavior (cf. Bandura & Walters, 1963), and it may be that their parents display the greatest consistency in disapproving of cheating.

All this does not mean, of course, that the parent should impose strict, unyielding restrictions on his child or establish unrealistically severe standards for him. The restrictions and demands must be within the child's abilities and should be sufficiently free to permit him to satisfy (to some degree, at least) his developing needs for independence. The parent's demands must be enforced, but they should be enforced with understanding and affection, not punitively, and the parent must be consistent.

Resistance to Temptation

We now come to the "payoff." If moral judgments and values are of any practical significance, they must obviously govern behavior in some way. How do an individual's moral values affect his actions? What conditions determine whether he will behave in a socially responsible, moral fashion or whether he will lie, cheat, or otherwise act unethically in order to gain his ends? Suppose that a person is given an opportunity to satisfy his desires through some socially disapproved action; what determines whether he will resist this temptation or give in to the lure of the easy transgression?

Many people do at times succumb to the temptations of minor (or even major) sins. The Hartshorne and May research of thirty-five years ago found that many children are honest in one situation but dishonest in another, similar setting. We must not exaggerate the degree of inconsistency here; some people are rarely dishonest, and others lie or cheat readily. Many of us transgress on a few occasions, even though we act in a thoroughly moral manner most of the time. Why do these moral lapses occur?

Youth and incomplete moral learning are not the whole answer. Adults fall prey to occasional temptations, just as children do. In a recent study of cheating by presumably adult college students (Hetherington & Feldman, 1963), only 41 per cent of the students in a course were never observed to cheat during the semester, and only 24 per cent of those who had transgressed at all cheated on all three examinations. These students were old enough to have developed stable patterns of morality (or of immorality), but the behavior of many still varied a little from one situation to the next. There is no simple explanation for these occasional falls from grace, but let us consider several of the factors that appear to affect an individual's resistance to temptation.

Fear-supported morality. First, we must acknowledge that a good deal of morality is supported by fear—fear of disapproval or of some other form of punishment. People often do the "right" things or avoid misbehaving because of external conditions (cf. Aronfreed, 1961). External factors determine, not only their judgments of the propriety of given actions, but also tell them what are their chances of being punished if they do misbehave.

Other people involved in the same situation sometimes lessen a person's fear. He may believe that these others will help him escape punishment. Even if he does not think of escaping penalty, the presence of others may reduce anxiety enough for the fear of punishment to become weaker (Schachter, 1959). Or, if there are a great many other people around him, he may feel anonymous and, therefore, think it is safe to carry out the socially disapproved action; with so many others present, surely *his* behavior cannot be detected.

Festinger, Pepitone, and Newcomb (cited in Berkowitz, 1962, p. 85) have pointed out that this feeling of anonymity may help account for much of the riotous activities of convention-goers. These people are away from their homes in a city where no one knows them and where they are part of a large and perceptually homogeneous mass. They can therefore indulge in activities which they would normally suppress. The psychologists have shown that college males assembled in groups are less inhibited in saying derogatory things about their parents when the students seemed to feel anonymous in these groups. The strength of their inhibitions against attacking their parents (and probably against other forms of socially disapproved behavior as well) is partly determined by the extent to which they see themselves as being lost in the crowd. The anonymous person does not have to be afraid of punishment and, consequently, need not keep to the straight and narrow path of morality.

Even if his fear is not lessened in the company of others, a person may still feel obliged to follow their illegal actions if they insist on such behavior and if he wants to gain their approval. A young boy may join a gang in robbing a store because he wants to keep the friendship of the other boys and does not want to appear "chicken." His fear of disapproval by the attractive group being stronger than his fear of being punished by law-enforcing agencies, the boy is impelled to do what his gang prescribes.

The strengths of conflicting motives. The preceding example leads us to another set of factors that affect resistance to temptations: strong desires may overcome moral values or may overshadow the fear of being punished for deviating from social standards. Sociologists—Durkheim, Merton, and Cohen —have this principle in mind when they suggest that regulatory social norms are frequently disrupted under the pressure of strong, unfulfilled wishes.

It is easy to see why such a moral breakdown would occur. For one thing, the desire to attain a particular goal may be stronger than the desire to adhere to a given value. A boy who is afraid of failing a test may want to pass this examination more than he wants to avoid cheating. He may then copy from his neighbor's paper if he gets the opportunity and is not fearful of being caught. The moral value is just not strong enough to counteract the intense opposing drive.

In addition, we may note that, in many cases, moral values and even the fear of punishment do not operate, to any great extent at least, without awareness. In these instances, a person has to know that a certain action departs from his own standards of conduct or that he is likely to suffer punishment for misbehaving if he is to resist the lure of the transgression. His strong yearnings can divert his attention. He does not think of how the given action might be wrong or how it might get him into trouble. All he knows is that he wants to reach his goal—to pass the examination, to have a car, to appear prosperous.

The person who is blocked from satisfying his desires is particularly likely to forget about his moral standards or to disregard the possibility of being punished. His frustration has probably strengthened his thwarted drive (cf. Amsel, 1958; Brown & Farber, 1951), and, furthermore, being emotionally aroused, he is less attentive to the peripheral cues that would activate his standards or his fears (Easterbrook, 1959). He becomes even more concerned about getting what he wants and pays less heed to other considerations.

One other possibility should also be mentioned. Moral values must at times be supported by commands that the individual gives himself. Suppose that a person finds a $100 bill on the street. Whether he will take the money to the nearest police station may depend in part on what he tells himself to do. The person often gives himself signals that put his moral standards into operation. The philosopher George Herbert Mead had such a phenomenon in mind in his analysis of social norms. He maintained that, in many cases of conformity to social standards, the individual holds an internal conversation with himself in which one part of the personality takes the role of the "generalized other" (society) and controls the individual's actions by means of covert verbal responses. He talks to himself in a sense and says, "Do this!" or "Don't do this!" Such self-signaling may be less likely to occur under the press of strong drives.

People who have often been thwarted in a given area of endeavor or who are for other reasons uncertain that they can reach their goals only through moral actions should therefore be prone to violation of moral standards. The more they want something and the less certain they are of getting it, the greater is the probability that they will think of nothing but their desires. This is one reason why duller students tend to cheat more frequently than their brighter peers (Hartshorne & May, 1928) and why there is more deceit in connection with difficult than with easy examinations (Howells, 1938). If a youngster wants very much to pass an examination and is afraid he might fail—either because of his intellectual dullness or because of the difficulty of the test—he may well forget about everything but passing the test. He may not stop to think that cheating is wrong or that the teacher might catch him transgressing, and he does not tell himself not to look at his neighbor's test paper. Concentration of attention on the primary goal crowds the secondary values out of the field of awareness.

If this analysis is correct, we now have one explanation for the inconsistent findings in studies of the antecedents of resistance to temptation (cf. Hoffman, 1962). MacKinnon's (1938) pioneering investigation found that the fathers of college men who cheated on a test had tended to rely primarily on physical punishment, rather than psychological techniques, in disciplining their sons. Other studies, however, have not obtained the same results. Putting the matter simply, we can say that the right kind of child rearing is a necessary but not sufficient condition of resisting temptations. Psychological disciplinary methods may foster the growth of moral values (assuming that the parents also possess such values), but whether these moral values are operative and controlling depends on other factors in the situation. The values may have been functioning in MacKinnon's psychologically reared students—perhaps because their desire to pass the test was relatively weak or because they saw a good chance of passing on their own—whereas these moral standards may not have been salient for the psychologically disciplined subjects in other studies. At the time they were observed, their desires were conceivably just too strong.

Ability to defer gratification. Strong desires can be to some extent controlled. There are people who are capable of postponing their pleasures, as we saw in the section on achievement motivation, pages 35 to 36. In essence, these people act as if they tell themselves: "Don't mind not reaching your goal right now. You can get there at some other time." They might not cheat on an examination, then, if they thought that there were a probability of their not passing this particular test, because they are not insisting on the gratification of a successful test performance at a given moment. They can wait until the next time, when they might do better. Similarly, a boy who wants an attractive toy or a piece of candy but who does not have the money for it may not be tempted to steal if he is able to defer his pleasures. He can wait until some other time, when he might have the purchase price.

Criminal and delinquent behavior can be partially explained as a lack of this ability to postpone immediate gratification for the sake of delayed rewards. Many (but certainly not all) lawbreakers have not learned to put off their pleasures. More or less, they have to take when they think the taking is good. These people can probably refrain from stealing if they know definitely that they will be caught, but otherwise they are unwilling (or perhaps unable) to postpone their pleasures sufficiently to work and earn money legitimately.

Mischel (1961a) tested this formulation by asking a large group of Trinidadian adolescents whether they preferred to get a small piece of candy immediately or a larger piece sometime in the future. He found that the juvenile delinquents were most likely to insist on the smaller, immediate reward. Mischel's results also suggest that the ability to defer one's pleasures is involved in a relatively wide range of socially responsible behavior. The youngsters choosing the larger, delayed reward in general scored higher on a scale designed to measure habitual responsibility. As Benjamin Franklin put it: "He that can have patience, can have what he will."

The person preferring immediate gratification lives primarily in the present. Juvenile delinquents are apt to construct stories covering shorter spans of time than do demographically comparable nondelinquent boys (Barndt & Johnson, 1955). Many delinquents (and probably many adult criminals as well) are apparently oriented within a relatively narrow period of time. They think only of having their pleasures now, not of giving sufficient attention to the future.

Authorities sometimes describe the ability to postpone gratifications as a manifestation of "ego strength" or "ego controls." A person having a strong ego is supposed to be able to put off obtaining pleasures if he thinks that it is to his future benefit to do so; in short, he is better able to deal with a frustration than is the individual with a weaker ego, and he is less likely to display an emotional reaction to the thwarting. In one study (Block & Martin, 1955; cited in Berkowitz, 1962, p. 277), the psychologists assessed ego control in nursery school children by means of two tasks, one of which used the ability to defer immediate gratification in order to obtain a greater reward in the future. The investigators demonstrated that the children with strong ego controls exhibited more constructive play and showed less aggression following a frustration than did their undercontrolled peers. Being less insistent on getting their preferred pleasures right away, the former were less disturbed when they could not at once satisfy their desires.

Many highly aggressive youngsters seem to have weak egos in this sense. Redl and Wineman (1957) portrayed a group of hyperaggressive boys as having, among other things, a low frustration tolerance and a low resistance to temptation. They apparently wanted their pleasures as quickly as they could get them. When frustrated, they displayed intense emotional reactions. Many people who are aggressively antisocial seem to have somewhat similar characteristics. Unable to postpone the satisfaction of their desires for long, they cannot establish the inhibitions necessary to control and regulate their behavior in a socially adequate fashion; they are easy prey to temptations.

Socially responsible behavior clearly requires some degree of restraint and self-control. The theorists of self-actualization have not given sufficient attention to how such inner controls can be achieved. Indeed, having observed only people suffering from excessive inhibitions, they neglect the necessity of teaching children to impose *some* restraint on their desires. Too much inhibition may be bad, but there can also be unfortunate consequences—for the individual and for society—if inhibitions are too weak. Children must learn to put off their pleasures at times in the interests of obtaining future benefits—a learned attitude, without which they would be unwilling to undergo the education and training necessary to achieve technological competence and status. They would, moreover, be unable to function effectively in face of the inevitable frustrations of social life.

It may well be that prior frustrations affect a person's present ability to defer gratification. Mischel (1961a) suggested that a person would be more willing to postpone his pleasures in order to obtain future rewards if he has learned to expect such rewards at some time in the future. A history of frequent and severe frustrations could well cause the individual to lose almost all hope; anticipating being thwarted again, he wants to take his pleasures while he can get them. Nevertheless, the ability to defer gratification probably depends on more than the absence of extreme frustrations in the individual's past (cf. Bandura & Walters, 1963). The person has to learn when gratifications should be postponed, when they can properly be obtained, and what the appropriate channels for getting particular pleasures are. Adult intervention is undoubtedly involved in this learning, perhaps through the imposition of adult standards, direct adult teaching, and the influences of modeling.

Suggesting the importance of adult intervention, Mischel (1961c) has also reported that boys whose fathers were absent from the family were less inclined to postpone gratification than were those whose fathers were at home. Fathers may teach their sons to think of the future by setting goals for them, either explicitly or in a more subtle fashion, and by serving as examples for their boys. It may also be, as psychoanalytic theory contends, that a moderate acquaintance with frustration contributes to the ability to defer pleasure.

Whatever is involved in such learning, the conditions of child rearing that lead to the ability to postpone pleasures may be somewhat different from the conditions that foster the growth of moral values. It may be that the people who can resist both weak and strong temptations have actually been raised differently from those who are immune only to weaker lures. The former were presumably taught moral values as well as the necessity of occasionally deferring their gratifications, whereas the latter, having learned the difference between "right" and "wrong," had still not learned to postpone their pleasures in the interests of future rewards.

Conclusions

Although the evidence is not always strong and unequivocal, the pattern of findings is consistent. Parents who want their children to strive for excellence and to be responsible and law-abiding citizens must take an active part in training their children. They cannot concentrate solely on making the home an earthly paradise in which every childish desire is gratified, assuming that some mystical "growth process" will inevitably steer the child in the paths of truth and righteousness. Mothers and fathers who would cultivate achievement motivation and morality in their offspring must teach their children standards of excellence and proper conduct and with love and understanding make the youngsters want to live up to such standards.

The imposition of such standards is, however, often frustrating to the child. He must learn to suppress his desires and tolerate frustrations. Some acquaintance with thwartings is necessary in the development of such tolerance. In a word, the theorists of self-actualization have an oversimplified picture of child development. The child's personality is much more of a *tabula rasa* than they would have us believe, and parents must become involved in shaping this personality.

We may, indeed, also have philosophical misgivings about the doctrine of growth through gratification. Educators are now beginning to realize that this conception places far too much emphasis on individual self-indulgence and gives too little attention to the individual's relationship to his fellows and to society as a whole. A person must learn that he is involved with other people, that he has a responsibility to others, and that he must at times subordinate his wishes for the good of the majority. He cannot pursue his own happiness at all

times without concern for other people, even though he believes he is seeking self-fulfillment. His own wishes are no
unerring guide to morality. If everyone could formulate his
own moral standards without regard to the needs of others, we
would have, at best, anarchy. In his *History of Western Philos-
ophy*, Bertrand Russell notes that the romantic glorification of
the individual, emphasizing self-gratification unchecked by
social responsibility, is one of the cornerstones on which
fascism was built.

REFERENCES

Allinsmith, Beverly (1960). Directness with which anger is expressed. In D. R. Miller and G. E. Swanson, eds., *Inner Conflict and Defense*. New York: Henry Holt.

Allinsmith, Wesley (1957). Conscience and conflict: the moral force in personality. *Child Development, 28,* 469–476.

Amsel, Abram (1958). The role of frustrative nonreward in noncontinuous reward situations. *Psychological Bulletin, 55,* 102–119.

Aronfreed, Justin (1961). The nature, variety, and social patterning of moral responses to transgression. *Journal of Abnormal and Social Psychology, 63,* 223–240.

Atkinson, J. W., ed. (1958). *Motives in Fantasy, Action, and Society.* Princeton, N. J.: D. Van Nostrand.

Ausubel, D. P. (1952). *Ego Development and the Personality Disorders.* New York: Grune & Stratton.

Bandura, Albert, and F. J. McDonald (1963). The influence of social reinforcement and the behavior of models in shaping children's moral judgments. *Journal of Abnormal and Social Psychology, 67,* 274–282.

Bandura, Albert, Dorothea Ross, and Sheila A. Ross (1963). A comparative test of the status envy, social power, and secondary reinforcement theories of identificatory learning. *Journal of Abnormal and Social Psychology, 67,* 527–534.

Bandura, Albert, and R. H. Walters (1959). *Adolescent Aggression.* New York: Ronald Press.

Bandura, Albert, and R. H. Walters (1963). *Social Learning and Personality Development.* New York: Holt, Rinehart & Winston.

Barndt, R. J., and D. M. Johnson (1955). Time orientation in delinquents. *Journal of Abnormal and Social Psychology, 51,* 343–345.

Barry, Herbert, III, I. L. Child, and Margaret K. Bacon (1959). Relation of child training to subsistence economy. *American Anthropologist, 61,* 51–63.

Benedict, Ruth (1946). *The Chrysanthemum and the Sword.* Boston: Houghton Mifflin.

Berkowitz, Leonard (1962). *Aggression: A Social Psychological Analysis.* New York: McGraw-Hill.

Berkowitz, Leonard, and Edna Rawlings (1963). Effects of film violence on inhibitions against subsequent aggression. *Journal of Abnormal and Social Psychology,* **66,** 405–412.

Blum, G. S. (1953). *Psychoanalytic Theories of Personality.* New York: McGraw-Hill.

Boehm, Leonore (1962a). The development of conscience: a comparison of American children of different mental and socioeconomic levels. *Child Development,* **33,** 575–590.

Boehm, Leonore (1962b). The development of conscience: a comparison of students in Catholic parochial schools and in public schools. *Child Development,* **33,** 591–602.

Boehm, Leonore, and M. L. Nass (1962). Social class differences in conscience development. *Child Development,* **33,** 565–574.

Brim, O. G., Jr. (1959). *Education for Child Rearing.* New York: Russell Sage Foundation.

Bronfenbrenner, Urie (1958). Socialization and social class through time and space. In Eleanor Maccoby, T. M. Newcomb, and E. L. Hartley, eds., *Readings in Social Psychology* (3rd ed.). New York: Henry Holt.

Bronfenbrenner, Urie (1960). Freudian theories of identification and their derivatives. *Child Development,* **31,** 15–40.

Bronfenbrenner, Urie (1962). The role of age, sex, class, and culture in studies of moral development. *Religious Education—Research Supplement,* **57,** S 3–S 17.

Brown, A. W., Joan Morrison, and Gertrude B. Couch (1947). Influence of affectional family relationships on character development. *Journal of Abnormal and Social Psychology,* **42,** 422–428.

Brown, J. S., and I. E. Farber (1951). Emotions conceptualized as intervening variables—with suggestions toward a theory of frustration. *Psychological Bulletin,* **48,** 465–495.

Burton, R. V., Eleanor E. Maccoby, and Wesley Allinsmith (1961). Antecedents of resistance to temptation in four-year-old children. *Child Development,* **32,** 689–710.

Chase, Stuart (1931). *Mexico: A Study of Two Americas.* New York: Macmillan, 1931. Cited in D. C. McClelland, *The Achieving Society.* New York: D. Van Nostrand. Pp. 394 f.

Clark, J. P., and E. P. Wenninger (1962). Socioeconomic class and area as correlates of illegal behavior among juveniles. *American Sociological Review,* **27,** 826–834.

Cohen, A. K. (1955). *Delinquent Boys.* Glencoe, Ill.: Free Press.

Crockett, H. J., Jr. (1962). The achievement motive and differential occupational mobility in the United States. *American Sociological Review,* **27,** 191–204.

Davis, Allison (1944). Socialization and adolescent personality. In National Society for the Study of Education, *Forty-Third Yearbook: Part I, Adolescence.* Chicago: Department of Education, University of Chicago.

DeCharms, Richard, and G. H. Moeller (1962). Values expressed in American children's readers. *Journal of Abnormal and Social Psychology,* **64,** 136–142.

Dolger, Laura, and Janet Ginandes (1946). Children's attitudes toward discipline as related to socioeconomic status. *Journal of Experimental Education,* **15,** 161–165.

Douvan, Elizabeth (1956). Social status and success striving. *Journal of Abnormal and Social Psychology,* **52,** 219–223.

Douvan, Elizabeth, and Joseph Adelson (1958). The psychodynamics of social mobility in adolescent boys. *Journal of Abnormal and Social Psychology,* **56,** 31–44.

Durkin, Dolores (1959a). Children's concepts of justice: a comparison with the Piaget data. *Child Development,* **30,** 59–67.

Durkin, Dolores (1959b). Children's concepts of justice: a further comparison with the Piaget data. *Journal of Educational Research,* **52,** 252–257.

Durkin, Dolores (1959c). Children's acceptance of reciprocity as a justice-principle. *Child Development,* **30,** 289–296.

Dynes, R. R., A. C. Clarke, and Simon Dinitz (1956). Levels of occupational aspiration: some aspects of family experience as a variable. *American Sociological Review,* **21,** 212–215.

Easterbrook, J. A. (1959). The effect of emotion on cue utilization and the organization of behavior. *Psychological Review,* **66,** 183–201.

Fenichel, Otto (1945). *The Psychoanalytic Theory of Neurosis.* New York: W. W. Norton.

Freud, Anna (1937). *The Ego and the Mechanisms of Defence.* London: Hogarth Press.

Freud, Sigmund (1932). Why war? In James Strachey, ed., *Miscellaneous Papers, 1888–1938,* Vol. V of Sigmund Freud, Collected Papers. New York: Basic Books, 1959.

Freud, Sigmund (1933). *New Introductory Lectures on Psychoanalysis.* New York: W. W. Norton.

Fromm, Erich (1947). *Man for Himself: An Inquiry into the Psychology of Ethics.* New York: Rinehart.

Glazer, Nathan (1957). The American Jew and the attainment of middle-class rank: some trends and explanations. In Marshall Sklare, ed., *The Jews: Social Patterns of an American Group.* Glencoe, Ill.: Free Press.

Glueck, Sheldon, and Eleanor Glueck (1950). *Unraveling Juvenile Delinquency*. New York: Commonwealth Fund.

Goldstein, Bernice, and R. L. Eichhorn (1961). The changing Protestant ethic: rural patterns in health, work, and leisure. *American Sociological Review, 26*, 557–565.

Green, A. W. (1946). The middle-class male child and neurosis. *American Sociological Review, 11*, 31–41.

Harrower, Molly R. (1934). Social status and the moral development of the child. *British Journal of Educational Psychology, 4*, 75–95.

Hartshorne, Hugh, and M. A. May (1928). *Studies in the Nature of Character: I. Studies in Deceit*. New York: Macmillan.

Hetherington, Mavis, and S. E. Feldman (1963). College cheating as a function of subject and situational variables. (Unpublished study.)

Hieronymus, A. N. (1951). A study of social class motivation: relationships between anxiety for education and certain socioeconomic and intellectual variables. *Journal of Educational Psychology, 42*, 193–205.

Hoffman, M. L. (1960). Power assertion by the parent and its impact on the child. *Child Development, 31*, 129–143.

Hoffman, M. L. (1962). The role of the parent in the child's moral growth. *Religious Education—Research Supplement, 57*, S 18–S 33.

Hoffman, M. L., S. B. Mitsos, and R. E. Protz (1958). Achievement striving, social class, and test anxiety. *Journal of Abnormal and Social Psychology, 56*, 401–403.

Hollingshead, A. B. (1958). Factors associated with prevalence of mental illness. In Eleanor Maccoby, T. M. Newcomb, and E. L. Hartley, eds., *Readings in Social Psychology* (3rd ed.). New York: Henry Holt.

Howells, T. H. (1938). Factors influencing honesty. *Journal of Social Psychology, 9*, 97–102.

Hsu, F. L. K. (1961). *Psychological Anthropology: Approaches to Culture and Personality*. Homewood, Ill.: Dorsey Press.

Hyman, H. H. (1953). The value systems of different classes. In Reinhard Bendix and S. M. Lipset, eds., *Class, Status, and Power*. Glencoe, Ill.: Free Press.

Johnson, R. C. (1962). A study of children's moral judgments. *Child Development, 33*, 327–354.

Kagan, Jerome, and H. A. Moss (1959). Stability and validity of achievement fantasy. *Journal of Abnormal and Social Psychology, 58*, 357–364.

Katz, Daniel, and K. W. Braly (1933). Racial stereotypes of 100 college students. *Journal of Abnormal and Social Psychology, 28*, 280–290.

Kinsey, A. C., W. B. Pomeroy, and C. E. Martin (1948). *Sexual behavior in the human male.* Philadelphia: W. B. Saunders.

Kluckhohn, Florence R., and F. L. Strodtbeck (1961). *Variations in Value Orientations.* Evanston, Ill.: Row, Peterson.

Kohn, M. L. (1959a). Social class and parental values. *American Journal of Sociology,* **64,** 337–351.

Kohn, M. L. (1959b). Social class and the exercise of parental authority. *American Sociological Review,* **24,** 352–366.

Krebs, A. M. (1958). Two determinants of conformity: age of independence training and achievement. *Journal of Abnormal and Social Psychology,* **56,** 130 f.

Lefkowitz, Monroe, R. R. Blake, and Jane S. Mouton (1955). Status factors in pedestrian violation of traffic signals. *Journal of Abnormal and Social Psychology,* **51,** 704–706.

Lenski, Gerhard (1961). *The Religious Factor.* New York: Doubleday.

Lipset, S. M., and Reinhard Bendix (1959). *Social Mobility in Industrial Society.* Berkeley: University of California Press.

McArthur, Charles (1955). Personality differences between middle and upper classes. *Journal of Abnormal and Social Psychology,* **50,** 247–254.

McClelland, D. C. (1955). Some social consequences of achievement motivation. In M. R. Jones, ed., *Nebraska Symposium on Motivation, 1955.* Lincoln: University of Nebraska Press.

McClelland, D. C. (1961). *The Achieving Society.* Princeton, N. J.: D. Van Nostrand.

McClelland, D. C., J. W. Atkinson, R. A. Clark, and E. L. Lowell (1953). *The Achievement Motive.* New York: Appleton-Century-Crofts.

MacKinnon, D. W. (1938). Violation of prohibitions. In H. A. Murray, *Explorations in Personality.* New York: Oxford University Press.

MacRae, Duncan, Jr. (1954). A test of Piaget's theories of moral development. *Journal of Abnormal and Social Psychology,* **49,** 14–18.

Maslow, A. H. (1954). *Motivation and Personality.* New York: Harper & Brothers.

Mayer, A. J., and Harry Sharp (1962). Religious preference and worldly success. *American Sociological Review,* **27,** 218–227.

Merton, R. K. (1957). *Social Theory and Social Structure* (rev. ed.). Glencoe, Ill.: Free Press.

Middleton, Russell, and Snell Putney (1962). Religion, normative standards and behavior. *Sociometry,* **25,** 141–152.

Miller, D. R., and G. E. Swanson (1958). *The Changing American Parent.* New York: John Wiley.

Mischel, Walter (1958). Preference for delayed reinforcement: an experimental study of a cultural observation. *Journal of Abnormal and Social Psychology*, **56,** 57–61.

Mischel, Walter (1961a). Preference for delayed reinforcement and social responsibility. *Journal of Abnormal and Social Psychology*, **62,** 1-7.

Mischel, Walter (1961b). Delay of gratification, need for achievement, and acquiescence in another culture. *Journal of Abnormal and Social Psychology*, **62,** 543–552.

Mischel, Walter (1961c). Father-absence and delay of gratification: cross-cultural comparisons. *Journal of Abnormal and Social Psychology*, **63,** 116–124.

Moss, H. A., and Jerome Kagan (1961). Stability of achievement and recognition seeking behaviors from early childhood through adulthood. *Journal of Abnormal and Social Psychology*, **62,** 504–513.

Munroe, Ruth L. (1959). *Schools of Psychoanalytic Thought*. New York: Dryden Press.

Mussen, P. H., J. J. Conger, and Jerome Kagan (1963). *Child Development and Personality*. New York: Harper & Row.

Mussen, P. H., and Luther Distler (1959). Masculinity, identification, and father–son relationship. *Journal of Abnormal and Social Psychology,* **59,** 350–356.

Myers, J. K., and B. H. Roberts (1957). Some relationships between religion, ethnic origin and mental illness. In Marshall Sklare, ed., *The Jews: Social Patterns of an American Group*. Glencoe, Ill.: Free Press.

Payne, D. E., and P. H. Mussen (1956). Parent–child relations and father identification among adolescent boys. *Journal of Abnormal and Social Psychology*, **52,** 358–362.

Piaget, Jean (1948). *The Moral Judgment of the Child*. Glencoe, Ill.: Free Press (originally published by Harcourt, Brace in 1932).

Redl, Fritz, and David Wineman (1957). *The Aggressive Child*. Glencoe, Ill.: Free Press.

Rieff, Philip (1961). *Freud: The Mind of the Moralist*. New York: Doubleday (Anchor Books).

Riesman, David (1950). *The Lonely Crowd*. New Haven: Yale University Press.

Rosen, B. C. (1959). Race, ethnicity, and the achievement syndrome. *American Sociological Review*, **24,** 47–60.

Rosen, B. C. (1961). Family structure and achievement motivation. *American Sociological Review*, **26,** 574–585.

Rosen, B. C. (1962). Socialization and achievement motivation in Brazil. *American Sociological Review*, **27,** 612–624.

Rosen, B. C., and R. D'Andrade (1959). The psychosocial origins of achievement motivation. *Sociometry*, **22,** 185–218.

Schachter, Stanley (1959). *The Psychology of Affiliation*. Stanford: Stanford University Press.

Sears, R. R. The growth of conscience. In Ira Iscoe and H. W. Stevenson, eds., *Personality Development in Children*. Austin: University of Texas Press.

Sears, R. R., Eleanor E. Maccoby, and Harry Levin (1957). *Patterns of Child Rearing*. Evanston, Ill.: Row, Peterson.

Sewell, W. H. (1961). Social class and childhood personality. *Sociometry*, **24**, 340–356.

Sewell, W. H., A. O. Haller, and M. A. Straus (1957). Social status and educational and occupational aspiration. *American Sociological Review*, **22**, 67–73.

Siegel, Alberta E., and Lynette G. Kohn (1959). Permissiveness, permission, and aggression: the effect of adult presence or absence on aggression in children's play. *Child Development*, **30**, 131–141.

Simpson, R. L. (1962). Parental influence, anticipatory socialization, and social mobility. *American Sociological Review*, **27**, 517–522.

Straus, M. A. (1962). Deferred gratification, social class, and the achievement syndrome. *American Sociological Review*, **27**, 326–335.

Strodtbeck, F. L. (1957). Family interaction, values, and achievement. In Marshall Sklare, ed., *The Jews: Social Patterns of an American Group*. Glencoe, Ill.: Free Press.

Terrell, Glenn, Jr., Kathryn Durkin, and Melvin Wiesley (1959). Social class and the nature of the incentive in discrimination learning. *Journal of Abnormal and Social Psychology*, **59**, 270–272.

Veroff, Joseph, J. W. Atkinson, Sheila C. Feld, and Gerald Gurin (1960). The use of thematic apperception to assess motivation in a nationwide interview study. *Psychological Monographs*, **74**, No. 12 (Whole No. 499).

Veroff, Joseph, Sheila Feld, and Gerald Gurin (1962). Achievement motivation and religious background. *American Sociological Review*, **27**, 205–217.

Weber, Max (1930). *The Protestant Ethic and the Spirit of Capitalism*. New York: Charles Scribner's Sons.

Whiting, J. W. M. (1959). Sorcery, sin, and the superego. In M. R. Jones, ed., *Nebraska Symposium on Motivation, 1959*. Lincoln, Neb.: University of Nebraska Press.

Whiting, J. W. M. (1960). Resource mediation and learning by identification. In Ira Iscoe and H. W. Stevenson, eds., *Personality Development in Children*. Austin: University of Texas Press.

Whiting, J. W. M., and I. L. Child (1953). *Child Training and Personality: A Cross-Cultural Study*. New Haven: Yale University Press.

Wilson, W. C. (1960). Extrinsic religious values and prejudice. *Journal of Abnormal and Social Psychology,* **60,** 286–288.

Wolfenstein, Martha (1953). Trends in infant care. *American Journal of Orthopsychiatry,* **23,** 120–130.

Zuk, G. H., R. L. Miller, J. B. Bartram, and Frederick Kling (1961). Maternal acceptance of retarded children: a questionnaire study of attitudes and religious background. *Child Development,* **32,** 525–540.

INDEX